Index of Real-Data Applications*

*For a complete list of all the applications in the text, see the Index of Applications that appears immediately before the general Index.

Bing & Grøndahl
Christmas Plates
The First 100 Years

by Pat Owen

Landfall Press, Inc.
Dayton, Ohio
1995
Distributed by Viking Import House, Inc.

Other Books by Pat Owen
The Story of Bing and Grøndahl Christmas Plates
The Story of Royal Copenhagen Christmas Plates

Bing & Grøndahl Christmas Plates
The First 100 Years
By Pat Owen

ISBN 0-913428-76-0
Library of Congress Catalog Card Number 94-79448

To the memory of my mother,
Forrest Penn,
with love, admiration and gratitude.

Table of Contents

Acknowledgments

This book was made possible by the loving support, help and encouragement of the following people:

Jørgen Sannung, Director of Collectibles for B&G and RC in Copenhagen, and Paul Steffensen, President of Royal Copenhagen USA, both of whom provided great encouragement.

Lisa Larsen of the Royal Copenhagen Company in Denmark who helped tremendously by doing endless research in an effort to insure my manuscript be up-to-date and accurate.

Alex and Edith Kaye of Landfall Press who edited the manuscript and offered many helpful suggestions and who say they've learned a great deal about Denmark in the process.

Lorraine Stone of Viking Import House who has helped for many years by checking over the stories of the yearly plates.

M. V. (Buzz) Owen, my husband, who not only helped by being my severest critic but also by being understanding when I had to spend considerable time at the typewriter.

Bent Møller who first introduced me to Danish Christmas plates back in 1949. This introduction definitely changed my entire life as I became involved with Christmas plates as a hobby and as a business.

The many friends, family members and acquaintances who kept telling me that we needed a book to celebrate the First 100 Years of Bing & Grøndahl Christmas Plates.

To all the above, I send my thanks!

Foreword

Those fortunate collectors who discovered Bing & Grøndahl Christmas plates years ago know well that eager yearning to add "one more plate" to their treasured collection.

To some it matters less whether the addition be the next year's plate or an older admired one. Their love for these classic little blue and white porcelain vignettes of life and tradition is very deep.

Over the course of the past 100 years Bing & Grøndahl's Christmas plates have served as a mirror of the times, often depicting the way that life has been lived in Denmark throughout the century.

In some cases the plates have recorded history. Others reflected the beauty of Danish architecture over the millenia of Danish history.

Though many of the motifs represent traditional Christmas themes such as family gatherings and decorated trees and churches, others reflect changes brought about by technological progress.

We invite all collectors to stroll down memory's lane with us here through the pages of history, romance and light-hearted folklore as seen through the eyes of Bing & Grøndahl artists since 1895.

Above all, this book is a unique collection of the art of some of Denmark's leading painters, some of them self-taught, and the artistry of some of the world's best porcelain craftsmen. There is nothing like it elsewhere.

Paul Steffensen, President
Royal Copenhagen USA
White Plains, NY
December, 1994

Dear Bing & Grøndahl Collector:

Harald Bing, the originator of the world's first porcelain Christmas plate, would be quite surprised to learn how widespread is the acceptance of his idea today, 100 years later. He might even be astounded to know there are collectors in more than 70 countries around the world.

We at Bing & Grøndahl extend special thanks to those long-time, loyal collectors who have contributed so significantly to this event, the 100th anniversary of the world's first commercial Christmas plate.

It is a matter of great importance to us that in some families third and fourth generations continue the tradition started many years ago. It is our pledge to continue to produce in years to come only plates of the highest quality in furtherance of this tradition.

Bing & Grøndahl also believes that this comprehensive book, published on the occasion of the 100th anniversary of the world's first and most valuable Christmas plate collection, will add to your enjoyment and appreciation of the unique art it contains.

Sincerely yours,

Leonhard Schrøder, Managing Director
Bing & Grøndahl A/S
Copenhagen, Denmark
December, 1994

13

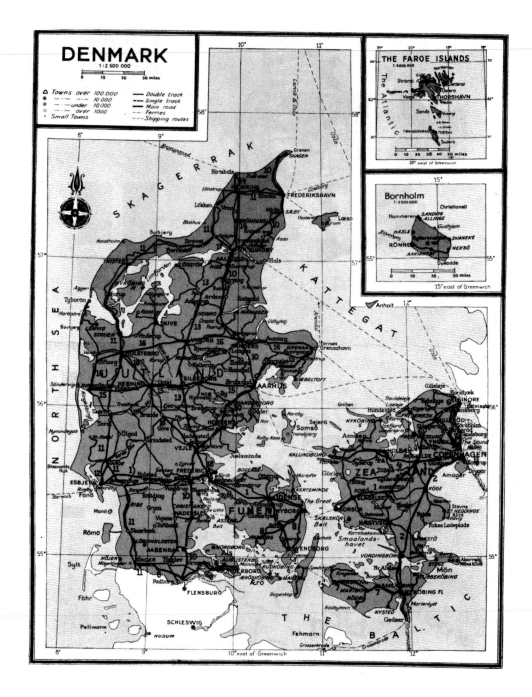

Introduction

Danish Christmas plates, in one form or another, have been a major factor in my adult life. How I first became involved with them is an interesting story in itself of foreign trade at the basic personal level. It illustrates how trade between nations fundamentally gets down to people. Here is just the short version of that story.

In 1948 I purchased the Viking Import House, a small gift shop in a Dayton, Ohio suburb, from Bent Møller, who had started the store for the sole purpose of selling Danish goods to Americans as a way to raise foreign exchange. The need to sell Danish goods was brought about by the fact that the Møllers owned a large office machine company in Copenhagen.

The Emilius Møller Company imported office machines from the United States, principally cash registers from The National Cash Register Company of Dayton. This was shortly after World War II and Denmark, like most European countries struggling to recover from the ravages of that war, would not permit its currency to leave the country.

Therefore, Bent had been commissioned by his father to buy up Danish goods with Danish kroner, sell them to Americans, and with the dollars received pay NCR for their cash registers.

Shortly after I purchased Viking Import House, and Bent had returned to Denmark, he wrote asking if perhaps I would like to try selling Danish Christmas plates. I asked that he send over a small assortment to let us see what they were like. Needless to say, I was immediately captivated by these lovely gems of Danish craftsmanship. And my life was changed forever.

Soon we were importing Danish Christmas plates by the thousands! At that time most could be had at the same low price. In the beginning we sold most annual issues at $6.00 retail but soon the price went up to $7.00 each. At one time, in the early 1950s, we had nine B&G 1895 plates in stock which we later sold at the unprecedented price of $50 each.

Today that price sounds unbelievable considering the price the plate brings now, but when it was first issued the 1895 plate sold for 50 cents! Since the demand gets greater every year, and the supply of old plates gets smaller, it is hard to imagine what the price may be in another 50 years.

Partly because I wanted to know more about Denmark, and partly because my customers were anxious for more information, I began to research and collect information on the historic places depicted on the plates. Our first several trips to Denmark involved discovering and visiting most of the places, buildings and monuments featured on the plates.

My husband and I have climbed a lot of towers and walked a lot of miles to learn as much as we could of the places written about in this book. Finally in 1961 *The Story of Royal Copenhagen Christmas Plates* was published, followed a year later by *The Story of Bing and Grøndahl Christmas Plates*.

Since that time, my husband and I, through Viking Import House, have been involved with collectibles, most especially with Danish Christmas plates. The company stocks all the new B&G and RC collectibles as well as many of the earlier issues. Viking recently started the VIDEX, a buy and sell marketplace which is proving very popular with B&G and RC collectors.

I have met thousands of collectors and shall always remember many of the stories they have shared with me about how much the plates have meant to them and what part they play in their family Christmas traditions. Many collections are handed down from parent to child, as is the tradition of awaiting the next year's plate.

Not long after publication of the two books, my husband and I were fortunate enough to realize two other long cherished dreams. A 40-foot sailboat was built to our specifications in Risør, Norway and we eventually sailed the *Viking* to the United States. The first leg of our odyssey took us to Copenhagen. The following year we sailed to Lisbon, Portugal and completed the journey to Miami, Florida the year after. Shortly thereafter we realized our second dream when we moved our home and business to Ft. Lauderdale.

Although we've kept the first two editions of the Christmas plate books up to date by adding a new page every year as the plates were issued, this book is the first complete revision of the Bing and Grøndahl story. It is only fitting and proper that it be published now for the 100th year of B&G Christmas plates.

Pat Owen
Ft. Lauderdale, FL.
December, 1994

The First 100 Years

Behind the Frozen Window
by
F. A. Hallin

1895

*W*hat motif could be more appropriate for the very first Christmas plate than the skyline of Copenhagen, so often referred to as the "City of Beautiful Spires"?

Through the frosted windowpane of the Frederiksberg Castle on Frederiksberg Hill the city's skyline is seen on a cold clear night. Frederik IV built the castle in 1704 as a summer residence. Today it is used as a school for training military officers. The government is currently restoring the castle to its former splendor and this restoration should be complete by 1996.

Along the skyline may be recognized, among other buildings, the contours of such famous structures as the Marble Church, the Round Tower with the Trinitatis Church, the St. Nicolai Church tower (the devastated spire was not reconstructed until 1909-1911), the Royal Stock Exchange and the Church of Our Lady (the Copenhagen Cathedral).

The history of each of these buildings is closely interwoven with that of Copenhagen. The city was founded in 1167 by Bishop Absalon who used three towers, a symbol of power, as his coat of arms. He called the fishing village Castrum de Hafn (Merchant's Haven) and shortly thereafter he built a fortified castle with three towers to defend it. The City of Copenhagen chose the Three Towers as its coat of arms, and in 1898 Bing and Grøndahl was granted permission to use the three towers as its trademark.

Copenhagen boasts many fine old buildings but the ones outlined on this plate are still among those most admired.

The southernmost of the Scandinavian countries, present-day Denmark includes the peninsula of Jutland, which extends north from Germany; two main islands, Zealand (on which Copenhagen is located) and Funen; and about 500 other islands. Greenland, the largest island in the world, is a Danish possession as are the Faroe Islands, 250 miles northwest of Scotland.

Not realizing how much the world would cherish these Christmas Plates, Bing & Grøndahl conservatively made only 400. Today this plate is much sought after by collectors and commands a very high price.

New Moon Over Snow-Covered Trees
by
F. A. Hallin

1896

*T*here is not a single acre of virgin forest left in Denmark. In the eighteenth century, when the wooded areas of the country had diminished to only four per cent of the total, the government began to recognize the threatening shortage of wood. It was then that strict laws were enacted to preserve Denmark's remaining forests. Had it not been for these laws Denmark would probably be without forests today.

The government has made it imperative that new trees be planted when an old stand is cut. It has also imported conifers and broadleaf trees from all over the world and years of experimentation have determined the trees best suited to Denmark's soil and climate.

Experiments with many foreign species of trees resulted in a keen interest in controlled harvesting of forest tree seeds. There have been established in recent years special tree nurseries to raise seeds from selected trees under controlled pollination. Denmark is also known for its techniques in selectively thinning forests. Those techniques, developed during the last century, are now widely followed in all European countries.

Currently about 1.1-million acres, or about 10.3 percent of Denmark's total area, are in forests. About one-fourth of this area is owned by the government.

Spruce and fir predominate in Jutland, the peninsula which contains the major portion of Denmark's 16,619 square miles, though beech can also be found there in abundance. The island of Funen, often called Denmark's garden, has many fruit trees in addition to willows and poplars. Beech and oak are the most common trees of Zealand, the large island where Copenhagen and Elsinore are located.

Christmas Meal of the Sparrows
by
F. A. Hallin

1897

*A*t Christmas, perhaps more than at any other time, we think of the animals and the birds of the fields and forests. This plate portrays the artist's conception of sparrows having their Christmas meal. The art also depicts an old method of twisting wheat stalks into a rope for binding a shock.

It is an ancient Scandinavian custom for farmers to put aside one sheaf of wheat from the harvest and to tie it to a pole at Christmastime to be a feast for the birds. Nowadays the city people also remember their feathered friends, especially at Christmas, by clearing snow from the window ledge and leaving bread crumbs for them.

Before 1880 Danish farmers devoted almost all their land to raising grain, particularly wheat, which was exported to European countries, principally England. Then in the late 1870s and early 1880s the vast new grain fields of North America began to provide stiff competition. Grain dropped to one-half its former price.

Danish farmers quickly realized it would be necessary to revolutionize their farming system if they were to survive. Within ten years they were concentrating on the raising of hogs, cows and chickens and now Denmark is noted for her exports of butter, cheese, bacon and eggs.

Grain, of course, is still grown in fairly large quantities. The progressive Danish farmer, through imported fertilizers and much hard work, has been able to increase the yield of his relatively poor acres to compete successfully with North American farmers. Even though three-quarters of the nation's total land area is devoted to agriculture Danish farmers do not now raise enough grain to meet the country's needs and much grain is imported every year.

Most Danish farms are small, about 42 per cent are less than 50 acres in size. About ten per cent of the farming area is planted in hay and the rest in grain and root crops, including cattle beets. These huge beets are high in sugar and protein and make excellent feed for livestock.

Christmas Roses and Christmas Star
by
Fanny Garde

1898

*P*erhaps the artist who made the original painting of this Christmas plate received her inspiration from the legend of the Christmas rose.

According to this legend, a little girl had accompanied her father to the fields on the night when an angel appeared before the shepherds to tell them that a Savior had been born in Bethlehem (see 1911 plate story). The older shepherds went at once to find the newborn babe and the little girl followed them.

When they arrived at the stable the little girl watched as the Wise Men presented their fine gifts and the shepherds gave their humble ones to the Christ Child. She cried softly because she had nothing at all to give.

She longed for anything -- even a flower -- but, alas, there were no blooming flowers. Then the little girl gave the only gift she could: she offered a prayer that God would bless the Mother and the Child. As she prayed, suddenly roses appeared where her tears had fallen.

She gathered them quickly and gave them to the Christ Child who immediately turned his attention from the gems and gold of the Wise Men to the lovely roses. Then he smiled at the little girl who had given him the gift of love and the first Christmas roses.

Another legend claims that what we call Christmas roses bloomed first in the Garden of Eden where they were known as Roses of Affection.

The U. S. Department of Agriculture believes that the Christmas Rose is native to Great Britain and may have arrived in Denmark courtesy of the Vikings. In any event, the plant retains the habit of blooming around Christmastime. Frost and snow seemingly do not deter the blooming; the blossoms are usually white, turning a pale pink when they begin to fade.

The Crows Enjoying Christmas
by
Jens Peter Dahl-Jensen

1899

Crows are quite numerous in Denmark and because they are often a nuisance the farmers are usually at war with them. This plate shows two crows sitting on a snow-covered tree branch on Christmas Eve.

Perhaps they are aware that somehow the world is a little different on this one night of the year. Surely they have noticed and taken advantage of the sheaves of wheat put out on poles by the Danish farmers at this time of the year.

Other birds found in Denmark's wooded areas include the sparrow hawk, falcon, buzzard, jay, thrush and woodpecker. Among the garden visitors are the sparrow, tomtit, finch, starling, nightingale and pigeon.

Near the lakes and streams can be found wild ducks, among them red-breasted merganser, coot, grebe and teal; songbirds include the reed warbler. The oyster-catcher, dunlin, lapwing, curlew, ringed plover, gull and tern live on the beaches.

The scene on this plate is from the island of Als near southern Jutland. The structure in the background is the old Notmark Church, constructed in Romanesque style hundreds of years ago of granite boulders and consecrated to Our Lady. In the middle ages the choir was enlarged and a tower was added. The gables of this tower were placed north and south, as was the custom on the island of Funen.

Not far from the Notmark Church is Dybbøl Mill, shown on the 1947 Christmas plate.

The island of Als is famous for its large number of ancient burial places. In the state-owned forest of Bloomeskol is one of Denmark's best preserved cairns, dating back about 4000 years.

Church Bells Chiming in Christmas
by
Jens Peter Dahl-Jensen

1900

*T*his beautiful bell is located in the church tower of the Syv (Seven) Church, 18 miles west of Copenhagen, near the old city of Roskilde. This bell was cast in 1515 by Johannes Fastenove of the Netherlands, one of the finest bell founders ever to work in Denmark.

The ancient town of Roskilde was founded by King Roar about AD 500 and was the capital of Denmark until 1416. It was one of the richest towns in the nation when Denmark included virtually all of Scandinavia and a large portion of England as well.

It was the seat of the bishops who owned the great Roskilde Cathedral and also much of Copenhagen. The Protestant Reformation changed all that and Roskilde lost its former importance.

The Roskilde Cathedral, consecrated in 1084, is now regarded as Denmark's Westminster Abbey. More than 100 persons of royal blood, including 36 kings and Queen Margrethe I, are buried here. Harald Bluetooth, first Danish king to adopt Christianity, was the first king laid to rest here and Frederik IX, who died in 1972, was the most recent.

In Danish the word *Roskilde* means Roar's Spring and there are a number of springs in the town and surrounding territory. One of the most important is the *Maglekilde* which flows at 100 gallons per minute. Little wonder King Roar chose this place for his court.

In the Town Hall Square of Roskilde is a sculpture of the founder and his brother, Helge. The inscription on the pedestal when translated reads:

At the springs of Lejre
With pride I'll wear my crown,
Do justice to any man in my realm
And here I'll build my town.

In 1969 a museum was built in the city to house Viking ships and artifacts recovered from the bottom of Roskilde Fjord. According to legend, the ships had been sunk in 1412 to guard the long, narrow entrance to the harbor and prevent enemy ships from attacking the town.

The Three Wise Men from the East
by
S. Sabra

1901

*T*his plate could easily be an illustration for the story of the Wise Men as told in Matthew 2:1-11 of the Bible.

The Bible does not give the number of Wise Men, but Christian tradition has always set the number of the Magi at three, and named them Melchior, Caspar and Balthasar. Perhaps tradition has held that there were just three because three gifts were presented to the baby Jesus: gold, myrrh and frankincense.

A legend circulating in the middle ages in Persia, believed to have been the home of the Magi, gives a specific purpose for three gifts. According to this legend three Wise Men once went on a long journey to visit a newborn prophet. They wished to learn if the babe would become a god, an earthly king or a physician and they carried gold, frankincense and myrrh to determine this.

The Wise Men reasoned that if the child took the incense first, he would be a god. Should he take the gold first, he would be an earthly king. To take the myrrh first would indicate that he would become a physician.

In paintings and in plays the Wise Men have most often been depicted as presenting their gifts to the infant Jesus in the manger. Yet the Bible definitely states that the Wise Men entered a house to see a child. It is believed that the Holy Family moved from the stable to a house on the eastern slopes of the town before the Wise Men arrived. Today there is a Franciscan chapel where the house is supposed to have stood.

When Marco Polo visited Persia in the thirteenth century he made diligent inquiries about the Magi. He was told they had returned to their home city of Saba and later were buried in a beautiful tomb.

Interior of a Gothic Church
by
Jens Peter Dahl-Jensen

1902

*J*ens Peter Dahl-Jensen, creator of this Christmas plate, portrays his impression of a Lutheran Church at Christmas. The candlelight radiates a sense of peace in the lofty Gothic sanctuary.

Although Christianity first came to Denmark in 827 in the person of a Benedictine monk named Ansgar, it did not gain a strong foothold there until the 960 baptism of Harald Bluetooth, king from 940 to 985. He was the first Danish monarch to adopt Christianity. Ansgar, later known as the "Apostle of the North," had been sent to spread the gospel by Louis the Pure, emperor of France.

Catholicism was unchallenged until 1536. Then came the Reformation and Lutheran tenets took root and still govern the Danish church.

According to the Danish constitution, the Lutheran Church is the national church and, as such, is supported by the state. Its confessional scriptures are the Old and New Testaments, the three symbols of the primitive church (the Creed, the Nicene and the Athanasian symbols), the original unaltered Augsburg Declaration of Faith of 1530 and Martin Luther's Little Catechism.

Laws on matters pertaining to the church are enacted by the reigning monarch and the Folketing (Danish Parliament) like other legislation. The National Church is administered by the Ministry of Ecclesiastical Affairs. A proposal to give the National Church its own constitution has often been debated but has never been carried out.

The nation is divided into nine stifts (dioceses) each with its own bishop and archdeacon (bishop's assistant). Each diocese is sub-divided into parishes. There are about 1700 parishes, each with a church and a minister.

All ministers, with very few exceptions, hold a theological degree. Women were admitted to holy orders in the National Church in 1948, among the first Western churches to do so.

Happy Expectation of the Children
by
Margrethe Hyldahl

1903

Children in Denmark are the same as they are everywhere else. For weeks before Christmas they eagerly anticipate the season.

During December evenings they make decorations for the Christmas tree. They shop for gifts and try to keep what they bought secret until Christmas Eve. Christmas Eve is the big time for celebrating the holiday here. It is on this evening that the big Christmas dinner is eaten.

Perhaps the three children shown on this plate are thinking of that delicious Christmas Eve dinner and the exciting things that follow. (See story for 1909 plate.)

The traditional Christmas dinner in Denmark always begins with rice porridge served in a huge bowl with a piece of butter in the center and usually sprinkled with cinnamon. Sometimes, though, it is served with fruit juice or even sweetened beer over it. Somewhere in the porridge is an almond and everyone must eat porridge until it is found. The person who finds the almond gets a special gift called the almond present. In households with several children it sometimes happens that each child finds an almond and gets a special present. But whether there are children or not, it wouldn't be a Danish Christmas dinner without everyone first eating rice porridge.

Then comes the main course. The traditional dinner is truly a feast, and always includes roast goose stuffed with apples and prunes, small caramel-browned potatoes and red cabbage. While Americans like their fruitcake and the English their plum pudding, the Danes prefer to end their Christmas dinner with apple cake made with layers of bread crumbs, applesauce and jam and topped with whipped cream.

View of Copenhagen from the Frederiksberg Hill
by
Cathinka Olsen

1904

*T*his plate shows essentially the same view as the 1895 Christmas plate. Here, though, the skyline of Copenhagen is seen from outside Frederiksberg Castle instead of from behind a frosted window.

The time is only nine years later and the city's skyline is little changed except for the addition of the Town Hall, outlined on the right of the plate. The Town Hall, depicted more clearly on the 1930 plate, was still under construction in 1904 and was not officially inaugurated until 1905.

Frederiksberg is a municipality adjoining Copenhagen to the southwest. In a land where the highest point is only 585 feet above sea level, the Frederiksberg Hill is a significant landmark and, as can be seen from the painting on this plate, once offered a perfect view of Copenhagen.

On top of the hill is the main entrance to the Copenhagen Zoological Gardens, founded in 1859 and considered to be the finest and oldest in all Scandinavia. Here, within its carefully tended 25 acres may be found hundreds of species of mammals, birds, reptiles, amphibians, fish and invertebrates.

The Frederiksberg Park, containing many stately old trees and picturesque canals, is the largest and most pleasing of the royal gardens in the Copenhagen area. Beautiful Chinese pavilions have been built on some of the islets within the park.

Once, the people of Frederiksberg and Copenhagen promenaded in the park, dressed in their Sunday best or sat on the *Sladrebaenke* (gossip benches) in front of the statue of Frederik VI, the park's creator, who was very popular in his time. He often sailed in a barge on the canals, wearing an admiral's uniform while accepting the hearty and respectful greetings of his faithful subjects.

JULE·AFTEN·1905

Anxiety of the Coming Christmas Night
by
Jens Peter Dahl-Jensen

1905

*T*he graceful deer standing under a snow-laden tree is in the Klampenborg Deer Park (*Dyrehaven*). The artist has tried to let it symbolize the anxiety and the feeling of holiness that comes with Christmas. The deer is all alone, and in its solitude it senses that something unusual, something sacred has happened: Christmas has come.

In 1670 King Christian V enclosed 2000 acres a few miles north of Copenhagen for hunting purposes. Now the park is perhaps the most popular excursion place of the Copenhageners. Here herds of deer with many a majestic stag pasture peacefully, seemingly unaware that man is ever an enemy of their kind. They provide an enchanting view, especially when seen against the background of the *Eremitage Castle* (shown on the 1923 plate).

Some of the most beautiful woods in all Denmark may be found in the park. Tall birches are the most numerous but oak and fir are also found in great numbers. The deer have completely eaten away the undergrowth, giving the open wooded area a character of its own.

In the southern part of the Deer Park is *Bakken*, the largest amusement park in Northern Europe. In addition to the usual shooting tents, wheels of fortune and various rides normally associated with amusement parks, here are also found beer gardens, restaurants, a dance pavilion and an open-air theater where performances are sometimes given by members of the Royal Theater of Copenhagen.

Taxes levied by the state on the income from the amusement park are used for the upkeep of the forest and to feed the deer in winter.

Sleighing to Church on Christmas Eve
by
Jens Peter Dahl-Jensen

1906

*T*his Christmas plate pictures a farmer and his daughter on their way to church by sleigh. Once sleighs were very much in use in the remote parts of Denmark, but now better roads and the introduction of the automobile and other modes of transportation have made the sleigh obsolete.

The church shown on this plate is the Faarevejle Church in the northwestern part of Zealand. This otherwise typical village church has become famous because it contains a glass-topped casket that holds the remarkably well-preserved body of the Earl of Bothwell.

Mary, Queen of Scots, in 1565 married her cousin Henry Stuart, Lord Darnley. Soon thereafter James Hepburn, Earl of Bothwell, fell in love with Mary. In 1567 Lord Darnley was murdered and the Earl of Bothwell was accused of having something to do with the murder but was acquitted after a trial.

Bothwell then kidnapped Mary and made her his wife. The Scots were not pleased about this turn of events and Mary was imprisoned while Bothwell fled the country. First, he went to the Orkney Islands, of which Mary had made him Duke, and later to Normandy, where he was captured and then confined to Malmø Castle in southern Sweden.

The marriage was later dissolved by the Pope. In 1573 Bothwell was transferred to Dragsholm Castle and was imprisoned there until he died five years later completely insane. Bothwell's body was disinterred about 300 years later and was found to be in a fine state of preservation. It was placed in a glass-topped casket in the nearby Faarevejle Church.

The Dragsholm Castle was long used as a prison, but was blown up by the Swedes in 1659. It was restored about 40 years later. Now it is used as a hotel.

The Little Match Girl
by
Ingeborg Plockross Irminger

1907

*T*his Christmas plate illustrates one of Hans Christian Andersen's best-known fairy tales, *The Little Match Girl*. The story was first published in Copenhagen in 1846 in the *Dansk Folkekalender*. Andersen wrote this about the story:

"*The Little Match Girl* was written at the Castle of Graasten, where I stopped for a few days on a journey abroad, and where I received a letter from the publisher, Mr. Flinch, asking me to write a story for the almanac, to accompany one of three pictures enclosed. The picture I chose was that of a poor little girl with a bundle of matches."

The picture referred to by Andersen was a drawing by the Danish painter J. T. Lundbye (1818 - 1848).

The story took place on a bitterly cold New Year's Eve. The little match girl was afraid to go home because she had not sold even a penny's worth of matches all day and she knew her father would beat her. As she sat forlornly on the steps of a house she decided to try to warm herself by lighting one match.

The glow of the match made her imagine she was warming herself by a cozy stove. The illusion lasted only as long as the match burned. The second match caused her to think there was a delicious roast goose in front of her. With the third match she thought she saw a beautiful Christmas tree.

While burning the fourth match the little girl saw her grandmother, the only person who had ever loved her and who was now dead. In an effort to keep the image of her grandmother, she struck match after match. She begged her grandmother to take her along to the place where the grandmother went after each match burned.

The next morning the little match girl was found on the steps, frozen to death but with a smile on her face.

St. Petri Church of Copenhagen
by
Povl Jørgensen

1908

Copenhagen has many fine old buildings, but St. Petri Church is considered by many to be one of the most beautiful. Certainly it is one of the oldest churches in the city, with records dating back to 1304. It was devastated by fire in 1386 and again in 1728. Damage was once again inflicted in 1807 by a British fleet under Admiral Gambier, which after heavy action in the harbor of Copenhagen, took over the Danish warships to prevent their falling into the hands of Napoleon. Each time the building was restored.

From 1450 until the Reformation, St. Petri (St. Peter's) was a parish church. Then for several years it was used as a cannon and bell foundry. In 1574 it was adopted by the Germans living in the city and since that time has been known as the German Church of Copenhagen. In its present form the church dates back to 1816.

The attractive copper steeple shown on this Christmas plate was erected during 1756 - 1757. Inside the church are two silver candelabra given by Queen Sofie Magdalene in 1731. Several monuments may be found in the surrounding gardens.

Diagonally across the street is another famous old church, the Church of Our Lady, which has served as Copenhagen's cathedral since 1924. The English bombardment destroyed the spire which was never rebuilt. Instead it was replaced by the cross seen today.

This church's facade has six tall columns flanked by bronze statues of Moses and David. Inside may be found Bertel Thorvaldsen's famous marble figures of *Christ and the Apostles*. A soft light glows behind the figure of Christ, showing the carved inscription *Kommer Til Mig* (Come Unto Me). It was here that many of the medieval kings were crowned, and since 1537 all the bishops, the chief dignitaries of the church, have been consecrated here.

Happiness Over the Yule Tree
by
Aarestrup

1909

*A*fter the Danish Christmas Eve dinner (see story for the 1903 plate) is over and the dishes are finished, mother and father disappear for a few minutes. Expectations are high at this point because everyone knows they are in the living room lighting the candles on the Christmas tree.

Mother and father then open the door with a smile and everyone rushes to see the beautiful tree which the children have not been allowed to see until this moment. Small wonder then that the little boy on this Christmas plate seems to be enthralled.

The tree is radiant with candles, tinsel, hearts, baskets filled with sweets, flags, and at the top is a silver star! Around the foot of the tree are all the gaily wrapped gifts. Before any gift exchanging takes place it is the custom that all join hands and dance around the tree, singing some of the old Danish Christmas songs.

Other favorites hymns include Stille Nat (*Silent Night*) and *Merry Christmas, Lovely Christmas.* Although this singing is definitely part of Christmas in Denmark, Christmas caroling, where the singers travel from house to house, is never done.

After the singing it is time for what the children have long and eagerly awaited -- the gift exchange. On Christmas Eve the children are allowed to stay up late and when they are finally tucked in for the night, with their Christmas gifts stacked at the foot of the bed, they are transported into a world of pleasant dreams.

Christmas Day is normally kept rather quietly. The family generally stays home and the children play with the toys received the night before.

The Old Organist
by
C. Ersgaard

1910

*P*ractically all Danish churches have an organ and some of the players are internationally- known musicians. The organ shown on this Christmas plate is probably in a medieval church. The dress of the organist is also indicative of the Middle Ages.

Organs go far back into history. It is known they were fully developed at the time of Christ. Hero of Alexandria described an organ in his *Pneumatica* about 100 BC. Tertullian mentions a certain Ctesibus as the inventor of the organ, and Archimedes as the man who put the finishing touch on it.

According to the Spanish Bishop Julianus (about AD 450) the organ was first found in Europe in the Spanish churches. It was first heard of in France in AD 757 when Emperor Pepin the Little is said to have received an organ as a gift from the Byzantine emperor. Organs came to Denmark during the period of Catholicism.

The art of organ building is at a high level in Denmark. In 1961 the organ of the Swedish town of Kristianstad (named after its founder, Christian IV of Denmark) was rebuilt in its original style by a Danish organ builder.

The design of the beautiful Grundtvig Church, in the northwestern part of Copenhagen, was inspired by the symmetry of a church organ and the simplicity of the Danish village churches. It is considered one of the world's masterpieces of contemporary religious architecture.

One of Denmark's most famous organs is in the castle church at Frederiksberg. Called the Compenius Organ, it was built in 1634 and is still in its original state and very much in use.

The Danes have always been fond of music and most homes have some sort of musical instrument. The people of Copenhagen can hear good orchestras at reasonable prices. Foreign operas are performed in Danish at the Royal Theater.

First It Was Sung by the Angels to the
Shepherds in the Field
by
H. Moltke

1911

*T*his plate depicts the angel appearing before the shepherds at the time of the birth of Christ. Many historians believe that Christ was born in the springtime because the shepherds were watching their flocks by night, which they did not ordinarily do except during the season when the lambs are born.

And in that region there were shepherds out in the field, keeping watch over their flock by night. And an angel of the Lord appeared to them, and the glory of the Lord shone around them, and they were filled with fear. And the angel said to them, "Be not afraid; for behold, I bring you good news of a great joy which will come to all the people; for to you is born this day in the city of David a Savior, who is Christ the Lord. And this will be a sign for you: you will find a babe wrapped in swaddling cloths and lying in a manger." And suddenly there was with the angel a multitude of the heavenly host praising God and saying, "Glory to God in the highest, and on earth peace among men with whom he is pleased!"

When the angels went away from them into heaven, the shepherds said to one another, "Let us go over to Bethlehem and see this thing that has happened, which the Lord has made known to us." And they went with haste, and found Mary and Joseph, and the babe lying in a manger. And when they saw it they made known the saying which had been told them concerning this child; and all who heard it wondered at what the shepherds told them. But Mary kept all these things, pondering them in her heart. And the shepherds returned, glorifying and praising God for all they had heard and seen, as it had been told them. (Luke 2:8-20, Revised Standard Version)

Going to Church on Christmas Eve
by
Einar Hansen

1912

*T*he parishoners in this scene are entering Ejby Church for the Christmas Eve service. The town of Ejby is located southwest of Copenhagen and a little northwest of Køge. The church, originally known as Munke-Ejby, was taken over by the Crown after the Reformation.

In 1604 the church was given to Henrik Gjøe, and among the subsequent owners were Corfitz Ulfeldt and Leonora Christina. It was taken from this couple, along with all their other possessions, when Ulfeldt was convicted of high treason.

Leonora Cristina, daughter of King Christian IV, spent 22 years of her life in prison because of her marriage to Ulfeldt. She was 15 when she married him. Copenhagen erected a Pillar of Shame (*Skamstøtte*) to Ulfeldt, the most notorious and most hated traitor in Danish history. The *Skamstøtte* may still be seen in the National Museum.

The Ejby Church is just one of several typical Danish village churches depicted on Christmas plates. The pride of the Danish people in their village churches is justified as 90 per cent of their churches are over 700 years old. During the twelfth and thirteenth centuries there were some 1700 to 1800 churches erected, many of which are still in use.

Up to the middle of the nineteenth century membership in the Lutheran Church was compulsory for Danish subjects. Catholics, Reformists and Jews had residential rights in certain towns. The Constitutional Act of 1849 introduced full religious freedom. Compulsory baptism was later abolished, and civil forms of marriage and burial allowed.

Today only the monarch must profess the faith. The people are free to worship as they choose, provided it is not contrary to public morality and good order.

Bringing Home the Yule Tree
by
Peter T. K. Larsen

1913

Conifers such as Norway spruce, Scotch pine, larch and silver fir were first cultivated in Denmark in the late eighteenth century. But the custom of using a tree as a symbol of Christmas was first introduced to the Danish people in the early part of the nineteenth century.

Nowadays every home in Denmark, however poor the family, must have its own Christmas tree. In addition to supplying the home market, Denmark now exports about 20-million Christmas trees every year.

Outside the larger cities it is still not unusual for a man to cut down a tree from his own land, as the man has done on this Christmas plate. Often the entire family participates in the selection of the tree, after which it is cut down and carried or pulled home on a sled.

Not only is there a tree in every home, but one is also placed in every hospital, hotel, restaurant and store in Denmark. The story for the 1930 Christmas plate mentions the gigantic tree found each year in the Town Hall Square of Copenhagen. Most of the other cities and towns also set up a Christmas tree somewhere near the heart of the municipality.

Whenever Danish ships start on a voyage that will keep the sailors away from home at Christmastime, a small tree is usually taken along. Then at Christmas the tree is placed at the top of the mast, and the holiday is celebrated at sea.

Even though the Danish yachtsman may get little use of his boat during the winter months, he likes to decorate it at Christmas. He often thinks it as necessary to have a tree tied to the top of his ship's mast, or atop the ship if there is no mast, as it is to have one within his home.

The Royal Castle of Amalienborg, Copenhagen
by
Peter T. K. Larsen

1914

*T*he Amalienborg, made up of four huge almost identical palaces, is the home of the Danish royal family. Among the finest examples in Europe of the rococo style, the buildings enclose an octagonal square in the heart of Copenhagen.

The arrangement of the buildings in the square is pleasing and arresting. The harbor and masts and rigging of passing ships can be seen between two palaces when looking in one direction, and in the opposite direction is seen Marble Church and its gleaming copper dome resembling St. Peter's in Rome.

Land for the magnificent edifices was given by Frederik V to four relatives with the stipulation that they employ the noted architect Niels Eigtved to build their palaces. Constructed between 1750 and 1760, the Amalienborg is considered by many to be the finest of the memorials that king left behind.

Frederik V never lived here as he and his court preferred the Christiansborg. But in 1794, when the Christiansborg burned, the Amalienborg was purchased to house the king and members of the royal family and it has been the official residence of Danish sovereigns ever since.

In the center of the court is a statue of Frederik V, considered by experts to be the finest equestrian statue in northern Europe. The statue was presented to Frederik V in 1770 by the Asiatic Company, which almost became bankrupt as a result. It ran into unexpected great costs when the sculptor, Frenchman Jacques Saly, became so fond of Copenhagen that he deliberately protracted his work to prolong his stay there.

Another famous equestrian statue is that of Christian V, located in the center of *Kongens Nytorv* (King's New Market), Copenhagen's largest square. Students who are graduating, or who have just graduated, come here every June in quaint yellow horse-drawn wagons to celebrate the end of the school term. They join hands and circle the statue three times shouting their Danish "hurrahs."

*The Chained Dog Getting a Double Meal
on Christmas Eve
by
Jens Peter Dahl-Jensen*

1915

*I*n Denmark, as in many countries of the world, dogs have been popular pets for many generations.

On this Christmas plate is shown a dog, chained to his doghouse, watching his master's home on Christmas Eve. Through the window he can see the Christmas tree and he has probably sensed the excitement of the season. Surely he must realize this is a very special night.

The family has not forgotten its canine friend for in the bowl beside him is a double ration of food. It is an old Scandinavian custom that all pets, as well as the farm animals, get double rations on Christmas Eve.

Although large, the dog shown is of an undefinable breed. The artist deliberately painted him this way to portray a common dog rather than one of the popular breeds. It is now illegal in Denmark to keep a dog chained in this fashion, even though it be well-treated by its family.

Everyone owning a dog in Denmark, and many people do, must buy a dog tag each year. Dog owners are also required to carry liability insurance.

More than 108 breeds of dogs are recognized by the Danish Kennel Club. Among the most popular are the Alsatian, the Labrador and the Golden Retriever. Of course, there are many thousands of dogs, in town and country alike, that are just as loved and admired but do not qualify for registration papers because of mixed breeding.

Christmas Prayer of the Sparrows
by
J. Bloch Jørgensen

1916

On the eastern coast of Zealand are chalk cliffs called *Stevns Klint*. While striking in appearance they are only about one-third as high as those on the island of Møn.

The Højerup Church depicted on this plate was built near the edge of *Stevns Klint* during the latter part of the thirteenth century. Legend says that after the church discovered its foundation was being undermined by the sea, it has moved itself a handbreadth inland every Christmas.

This retreat from the edge of the precipice must have been too cautious because the church cemetery, and in 1928 part of the church, toppled into the sea. In recent years the church has been restored and the cliffs below it reinforced with masonry to prevent future damage.

Church building in Denmark began on a large scale in the 1100s. The great majority of the hundreds of large and small churches erected all over the country at that time are in the Romanesque, or round arch, style.

Many of these early churches were built by the peasants themselves. They were constructed of granite collected on the spot and there rough-hewn in squares. About the year 1200 the Gothic, or pointed arch, style appeared in Denmark and this style of architecture continued, with some modifications, until the middle of the fifteenth century.

About a half century after the start of extensive church building, the supply of available granite began to run short. Valdemar the Great and Bishop Absalon then showed great foresight by summoning artisans from northern Italy to teach the Danes how to fire bricks and erect buildings from them. The brick industry still flourishes in Denmark.

Arrival of the Christmas Boat
by
Johannes Achton Friis

1917

*T*he "arrival of the Christmas boat" refers to the annual coming of a boat carrying Americans of Danish descent home to Denmark for the Christmas celebration. At the time this plate was crafted, all passenger boats coming from America after mid-December were considered Christmas boats and awarded special welcomes.

Upon arrival, the boat was gaily dressed with flags and bunting and there was a festive holiday spirit aboard. The harbor was likewise decorated for the season and bands played as the big passenger liner was guided to her berth by tugboats.

Many in the happy, smiling, waving crowd on shore must have wiped away a tear of joy as they waited to welcome friends and relatives. Even the newspapers carried the names, and sometimes biographies, of the passengers. The jubilation was general as even passersby frequently joined in the welcoming celebration.

The first sizable group of Danes bound for America crossed the ocean more than a century ago in search of new opportunities. Soon hundreds of families followed, most never to return. Between 1820 and 1972 nearly 362,000 Danish men and women emigrated to the U. S., all but 50,000 coming between 1870 and 1929. They settled in all parts of the country, the vast majority becoming citizens, and contributed greatly to our society. Today there are more Danes in America than in Denmark.

Shortly after World War I an organization called Danes Worldwide was formed whose objectives were to "strengthen the bonds between Denmark and Danes abroad and between them mutually." King Christian X became the league's patron as did his successor Frederik IX. Today the patron is Peter Heering and the organization has a summer convention each year. At that time Danes from all parts of the world gather in the great banquet hall of Kronborg Castle.

Also prominent in keeping homeland ties alive are the American-Scandinavian Foundation in New York, its Danish American Women's Association division and the Danish Brotherhood in America, a fraternal organization headquartered in Omaha.

The Fishing Boat Returning Home for Christmas
by
Johannes Achton Friis

1918

*T*hrough the ages fishing has been important to the economy of Denmark. Fishing grounds lie off the Danish coasts and in recent years a sea-going fishing fleet has developed operations in the North Sea, the Kattegat and the Baltic.

The foremost fishing town is Esbjerg, on the west coast of Jutland. Here may be found some four miles of quays and hundreds of fishing boats. Other important fishing ports include Skagen and Frederikshavn in the extreme northeast of Jutland.

Fishing boats range from rowboats and sailboats to large motor vessels equipped to remain at sea for long periods of time. A fishing boat typical of the time of this plate would be similar to the gaff-rigged North Sea cutter it depicts. Such a boat was usually operated by four men who worked on a profit sharing basis.

The work was hard, uncomfortable and often dangerous and resulted at best in wresting a meager living from the sea. The most common varieties caught by the Danish fishermen are cod, haddock, plaice, herring and eel.

Danes, a sea-faring people from the beginning of their history, have long felt a responsibility for conducting marine research and have contributed much to our present knowledge of fish and of the sea. One interesting bit of information that required several decades of research pertains to the freshwater eel, varieties of which are found in Denmark and in North America.

It was finally proven that these species breed in the Sargasso Sea between the West Indies and the Bermudas. Then the young of these two entirely different species, assisted by the ocean currents, migrate to the shores of North America and Europe, where they find their way up fresh water streams. After growing for several years they start the long trip back to the Sargasso, where they spawn and die.

Outside the Lighted Window
by
Johannes Achton Friis

1919

Once again (as in 1907) Bing and Grøndahl has selected a motif to illustrate the story of *The Little Match Girl* by Hans Christian Andersen.

There is little, if any, poverty in Denmark. This country was the first in the world to introduce efficient social services; it has had an Old Age Pension system since 1891. The basis of modern Danish social legislation is a group of laws passed in 1933 and usually referred to as the Social Reform.

These laws resulted in a system of social security which also includes vacations, workman's compensation, accident aid, child welfare and national health insurance through state-approved sick-benefit societies managed by the people themselves.

Today, all men and women over 67 are entitled to an old age pension. Most people are members of the labor union, and these persons can retire at age 60 if they wish to do so. Most municipalities have built special apartments for pensioners where they can live for a nominal rent.

The health societies provide free medical attention, many free hospital services, and medicines at greatly reduced prices.

Legislation has been passed which guarantees every wage earner an annual five weeks of vacation. Each employee has a vacation card. If he changes his place of employment, he takes his vacation card to his new employer who must honor the days of vacation left. Three of the five weeks must be given in the summertime.

The many social services provided in Denmark are financed through the national income tax. Danes pay about 43 to 50 per cent of their salaries in taxes.

Currently there is about 10 per cent unemployment in Denmark. If the unemployed are members of a labor union they receive pay from unemployment insurance. If they are not union members they receive a small allowance from the government.

Hare in the Snow
by
Johannes Achton Friis

1920

*T*he hare is one of the more common wild animals of Denmark and is found in almost every part of the country.

The swift, timid, long-eared mammal closely related to the rabbit, is one of the few creatures out and around during the winter snows. Always on the search for food, they can be seen foraging in the fields where not infrequently they themselves become prey. Vegetarians who live in underground warrens, they eat almost any kind of vegetation, which does not endear them to farmers.

Hares and rabbits have been the subject of many folktales. Among the best known are Aesop's famous race between the tortoise and the hare and Beatrix Potter's tale of the busy bunny in Mr. McGregor's garden whose escapades have been translated into many languages. American folklore includes Joel Chandler Harris' Uncle Remus Br'er Rabbit stories and a certain well-known movie cartoon character.

Though artist Johannes Achton Friis depicts a winter scene on this Christmas plate, the creature is frequently associated with Easter. One European legend tells of Eostre, Teutonic goddess of spring, who fashioned the first hare from a bird. Grateful for this honor, the hare laid eggs once a year at a spring festival to its patroness, a fitting symbol of fertility. And that allegedly is why we associate eggs and bunnies at Easter to this day.

Other small animals relatively plentiful in Denmark include the marten, squirrel, badger, mole, hedgehog, shrew, weasel and field mouse.

The wolf, once native to this area, now is extinct. The only larger animals remaining today are the deer and the fox. Deer, once kept in exclusive royal hunting preserves, today are kept in public parks. A number of deer also live wild in the Danish woods.

Pheasants are particularly prolific and along with partridges are often seen rising into the air when startled by a fox or other predatory animal. There are many other types of bird life in Denmark, most of which are mentioned in the 1899 Christmas plate story.

Pigeons in the Castle Court
by
Johannes Achton Friis

1921

Near the heart of Copenhagen is an island called *Slotsholmen* (Castle Island), surrounded on all sides by canals. Here is where fishmongers, members of Parliament, stockbrokers, flower merchants and even Supreme Court justices conducted their business.

This picturesque island is the home of Christiansborg Castle which houses the Danish *Folketing* (Parliament) and once was home to the Ministry of Foreign Affairs. The castle is the sixth structure to be built on the site.

The first, more fortress than castle, was built by Bishop Absalon in 1167 and its ruins can still be seen under the present building. From 1441 until a disastrous fire in 1794, the Christiansborg was the royal residence. Pictured on this plate is the Royal Chapel, connected to the castle by the Cavalier's Passage, and still the church of the Royal Family and the Danish Navy.

Entombed in the church are two of Denmark's greatest naval heroes. One is the almost legendary Peder Vessel of Trondhjem, who defeated Charles XII of Sweden during the Great Northern War. For his many exploits he was named *Tordenskjold* (Thunder Warrior) by King Frederik IV. The other is Niels Juel, victorious over the Swedish fleet at Køge in 1677.

The chapel is one of the masterpieces of the famous Danish architect C. F. Hansen who also designed the Supreme Court of Justice (*Højesteret*), situated between the Castle and the Royal Chapel in St. George's Court. The dome of the chapel is adorned with angels sculpted by Bertel Thorvaldsen.

Also found on *Slotsholmen* are the Thorvaldsen Museum, the Stock Exchange, the Museum of Armor and the Royal Library. The open air market where fish, flowers and fresh vegetables were sold at the time this plate was made, is no longer there.

Star of Bethlehem
by
Johannes Achton Friis

1922

When scientists try to explain the star of Bethlehem it becomes difficult because no one knows for sure when Christ was born.

It has now been proven that Herod, who was king at the time of the birth of Christ, actually died about four years before the year we consider to be that of Christ's birth. Archaeologists working in Ankara, Turkey some years ago uncovered an inscription listing the years in which orders were issued for tax collections.

Three of the dates correspond to our 28 BC, 8 BC and AD 14. Historians have ruled out the first as being too early and the third as being too late for the tax census which brought Mary and Joseph to Bethlehem. This would seem to indicate that Jesus was born in 8 BC, but in those days travel was slow and communications poor at the edges of the Roman empire and it could have taken one or two years for the edict to arrive and be complied with in Palestine.

The story of the 1901 Christmas plate tells of the Wise Men and the star. "The Wise Men from the East" were probably from a part of the world we formerly called Persia, and were priests of Zoroaster and believers in astrology.

They believed that the location of heavenly bodies, particularly the seven ancient planets, influenced the lives of human beings. It is now known, though probably not in that day, that once each 805 years Mars, Jupiter and Saturn appear in an extremely close group. Since this last happened in 1604, it would also have occurred in AD 799 and 6 BC. This could easily have been accepted by the Wise Men as the sign for which they had long searched the sky.

Many Christians prefer to think of the Star of Bethlehem as a miracle that cannot be explained. Certainly the important thing is not the star, but the Christmas story itself.

The Royal Hunting Castle, the Eremitage
by
Johannes Achton Friis

1923

*A*lthough Christian V enclosed the Klampenborg Deer Park for hunting purposes, it was Christian VI who built the small palace in the park called the *Eremitage* (Hermitage) or sometimes called the Royal Hunting Castle.

Designed by Laurids de Thura and built in 1736, the castle is Christian VI's finest existing edifice. It is situated in the center of Deer Park in a particularly beautiful area known as *Eremitagen Sletten* (Hermitage Plain). Being about 130 feet above sea level, the castle commands magnificent views of a large part of Northern Zealand and of the passing ships in the Sound.

The influence of Viennese baroque is shown by the fine marble chimney pieces, gilt carvings and ceilings. Numerous nude statues decorate the gracefully curving roof.

Herds of 100 and more deer can often be seen in the vicinity of the *Eremitage*. In all, there are more than 1200 fallow and red deer in the park, many of which are relatively tame.

The Hermitage derived its name from the fact that King Christian VI sometimes wanted to be alone. At such times he would have his meals sent down by dumbwaiter from the kitchen direct to his private dining room.

Some years ago, when Queen Elizabeth and Prince Philip of Great Britain paid a visit to King Frederik IX and Queen Ingrid, they lunched at Hermitage Castle.

The castle is still used by the royal hunting party at an annual hunt. On that day, the park is closed to the public, but on the other 364 days of the year it belongs to the Danish people.

In addition to the deer killed during this annual royal hunt, it is necessary for the park rangers to thin out the herd from time to time. They particularly try to limit the number of stags. Only one stag older than seven years of age is allowed to live. When that stag becomes 12 years old a member of the royal family comes to the park and shoots it.

Lighthouse in Danish Waters
by
Johannes Achton Friis

1924

*D*enmark has a large number of lighthouses for a country of its size. Excluding Greenland and the Faroe Islands, the land area of Denmark is 16,576 square miles, or about half the size of the state of Maine.

This land is made up of the peninsula of Jutland, which adjoins Germany, and approximately 500 islands of which about 100 are populated. A look at the map on Page 14 makes it easy to understand why it was necessary to erect many lighthouses and other aids to navigation.

The two largest islands are Zealand and Funen. Copenhagen, Denmark's capital and largest city, is on Zealand. On Funen is the city of Odense, famed for being the birthplace of Hans Christian Andersen. The Great Belt flows between the two islands. Depicted on this plate is the Sprogø Lighthouse on the island of Sprogø located in the Great Belt about midway between Korsør and Nyborg.

The Danes are now building a bridge from Zealand to Funen via Sprogø, to be completed in 1996. Under consideration in Parliament is a bridge linking Amagar (near Copenhagen) to southern Sweden. The longest bridge now is the two-mile Storström, pride of Danish engineering, connecting the islands of Falster and Zealand.

In the early part of the last century, navigation through the Sound (the water between Denmark and Sweden) was made comparatively safe but very little was done in the Great Belt because it was easier to levy customs and light dues on foreign ships at Elsinore. (See story for 1950 plate.) As shipping rapidly increased, however, lighthouses and other navigational aids were added in the western part of the country.

C. F. Grove, head of the Danish Lighthouse Service from 1852 to 1883, did much to modernize the lighthouses. He replaced the old-fashioned coal-burning lights with revolving reflectors. He also erected 24 new lighthouses at strategic points and placed eight lightships in Danish waters.

The Child's Christmas
by
Johannes Achton Friis

1925

*E*very married couple derives a special joy out of the first Christmas of their first-born child. It is true that the child is too young to understand why Christmas is celebrated -- too young to enjoy his gifts as he will during later Christmases, but he is not too young to give a new meaning to Christmas for the parents.

It is easy to imagine the thoughts of this young couple as they look at the child and his first Christmas tree. They are dreaming of later Christmases, later children, and they are rejoicing for the wonderful things this Christmastime has brought to them. It is a moment they will long remember.

Danish people have their big family dinner and gift exchange on Christmas Eve. Christmas Day is observed rather quietly but the following day, generally referred to as Second Christmas Day, is given over to gaiety and entertainment. Many people spend the day going from house to house to visit friends and to *skaale* or drink to their health. The evening is often spent at the theater.

Christmas is the oldest of Nordic festivals and it is steeped in tradition. Long before the birth of Christ, a pagan festival of several days duration was held around the shortest day of the year. Bonfires and offerings were made to appease evil powers and spirits, but even in that heathen era gentleness, gifts and peace were part of the celebration.

To this day some Christmas customs are not altogether free from the influence of the older heathen and early Christian traditions. Some old folks still remember when it was considered quite dangerous to venture out on Christmas night because it was believed that evil spirits roamed freely on that night.

Churchgoers on Christmas Day
by
Johannes Achton Friis

1926

*T*his plate's artist, Johannes Achton Friis, was inspired by the Haraldstad Church, situated in the town of the same name a few miles north of Ringsted in Zealand.

This church contains the body of the Danish nobleman Knud Lavard who was murdered in the woods of Haraldstad on January 6, 1131 while on a visit to his relative Cecilia, a daughter of King Canute the Holy, and her husband Earl Eric.

Legend persists that a holy spring with curative powers gushed forth on the spot where the crime was committed. In 1146 a chapel was built near the spring and in 1956-1957 a modern concrete Lutheran church was erected here and named for the murdered man.

About 92 percent of the population of Denmark belongs to the Lutheran church though far fewer can be called regular churchgoers. Other denominations include the Methodist, Roman Catholic, Orthodox Russian, Church of England and Baptist as well as many others. These churches are generally divided into two groups: the recognized and the non-recognized. The ministers of the recognized group have authority to perform ecclesiastical rites which have civil validity. The non-recognized group may use the chapels of the National Church for funerals, but their clergy may not perform legally valid marriages and baptisms.

The National Church is financed from funds vested in it in former times by Treasury grants as laid down by legislation and by taxes levied on members along lines similar to those which apply to income tax. Non-members may easily gain exemption from the church tax. The State pays the pastor's salary but generally the local congregation pays for the upkeep of the church.

Skating Couple
by
Johannes Achton Friis

1927

*F*rom ancient times, the Danes have been a rugged people known for their love of outdoor sports despite the sometimes inclement weather and since no one in Denmark lives more than 40 miles from the sea it is not surprising they have long participated in aquatic sports.

One of the favorite wintertime outdoor activities, enjoyed in Denmark for centuries, is ice skating as shown on this Christmas plate.

Soccer -- called football everywhere in the world but in the U. S. -- is the Danish national game. There are many football clubs scattered over the country which compete with each other as well as internationally. When the Danish team won the European Championship in 1992, the entire country celebrated with singing and dancing in the streets for several days. In 1986 the Danish team reached the final round of the World Cup.

Other sports at which the Danes do well in international competitions include skiing, rowing, swimming, sailing, badminton, tennis, handball, archery, fencing and road cycling. Since many Danish families do not own an automobile, cycling is more than a sport; it is a common mode of transportation for men, women and children.

Inasmuch as Denmark is relatively level (the highest hill is only 585 feet above sea level), cycling demands no heavy exertion and it permits the people to travel at what they feel is a reasonable speed. Everyone in Denmark rides a bicycle -- cabinet members and even bishops.

Although the desire to win at sport is great, Danes do not allow that to deprive them of enjoyment from the sport for its own sake. The Danish people participate in sport for the fun of it. Their love of fun and good humor is illustrated by the well-known story of the Dane who went to Norway to ski. As he was attempting to put on skis for the first time, a passing Norwegian tried to be helpful by saying, "You have those skis turned the wrong way." To which the Dane retorted, "Just how do you know which way I'm going?"

*Eskimos Looking at the Church of Their
Little Village in Greenland
by
Johannes Achton Friis*

1928

*T*he bonds between Scandinavia and Greenland go back to the hardy Vikings who made voyages to North America by way of Greenland 500 years before Columbus. The modern colonization of Greenland dates back to 1721 and the arrival there of the Danish missionary, Hans Egede. Egede must have been persuasive because virtually all of the island's population belongs to the National Lutheran Church of Denmark.

Greenlanders are largely descended from Eskimos who probably migrated from North America. The common language is still Eskimo, although Danish is taught in the schools and is widely used. It is interesting to note that Greenland's radio broadcasting system, which since 1958 can be heard in the entire inhabited area, can be heard and understood by North American Eskimos.

Greenland, self-governing under Danish protection, is the largest island in the world (Australia being considered a continent) and is about 50 times as large as the rest of Denmark put together. Five-sixths of its 840,000 square-mile area, however, is covered by a vast ice cap, much of it up to two miles thick. Only a relatively narrow, treeless coastal fringe is ice-free.

Most of Greenland's 40,000 people live in or near the capital of Godthaab. The island's economy is largely based on the sea. For many years seals were abundant and supplied most of the needs of the people. In recent years, though, the surrounding waters have become warmer and the seals have moved elsewhere. In their place came codfish in unparalleled numbers but, unfortunately, these are not as plentiful today as previously.

A few sheep are raised in the extreme southwestern portion of the island. There is also some mining of cryolite, zinc and lead.

Fox Outside Farm on Christmas Eve
by
Johannes Achton Friis

1929

*T*he farm shown on this Christmas plate is probably located in Northern Zealand or Eastern Jutland for it was in these two areas that a fox was most likely to be found.

The fox, acclaimed in legend as one of nature's sly and crafty creatures, once was the bane of farmers, raiding chicken coops and being a general nuisance. A small flesh-eater with a bushy tail, foxes are members of the dog family and have been immortalized in folktales around the world.

Today there are not many wild animals to be found in Denmark. The largest, outside of zoological gardens, are the red deer, the roe deer and the fox. Hundreds of years ago there were several other species of large animals in this area but either they have died out as the forests shrank making existence difficult for them, or they were killed before the current strict laws were passed to conserve the wildlife of Denmark.

Three-fourths of Denmark's land is under cultivation. The average farm in Denmark is small, 79 per cent are 125 acres or less, and is worked by the owner and his family; tenant farming being an exception. In many cases, however, the farmer owns only the buildings and pays an annual rent for the land which remains the property of the state. Most farmers raise livestock and the crops necessary to feed them.

Danish farming is well organized through co-operative associations owned and controlled by the farmers themselves. These co-ops have done much to help the farmers in marketing their products and maintaining the quality for which the Danes have become famous.

The government promotes agriculture by running experimental farms and by establishing high quality levels of exports such as Danish ham, bacon and dairy products.

Yule Tree in the Town Hall Square of Copenhagen
by
H. Flügenring

1930

*E*very Christmas season a tall beautiful tree is placed in front of Copenhagen's Town Hall in the *Raadhuspladsen* (Town Hall Square), the busy hub of the city.

It is here in this square that friends like to meet in the weeks before Christmas to admire the lovely tree, festooned with a myriad of lights and decorations, and to wish each other a joyous holiday season.

The Town Hall Square is the heart of Copenhagen's business and entertainment district. Second in importance is *Kongens Nytorv* (The King's New Market), center of the so-called aristocratic quarter with its embassies, legations, the Royal Theater and the more expensive, though older, apartment houses. These two important squares are connected by a mile-long series of five streets known collectively as the *Strøget* (the Stretch).

There are also other times of the year when Town Hall Square is the gathering place of large groups. On the night of a general election, crowds gather here to read election results posted on the front of the big newspaper offices. It was here that the people gathered on that wonderful, memorable evening of May 4, 1945, when the news came that Denmark was being liberated. An equally large crowd gathered here in 1992 when the Danish soccer team became the European champions.

Copenhagen often is called "the City of Spires." The Town Hall, the building to the right of the Christmas tree shown on this plate, has the distinction of having the highest tower in the city. It is 346 feet high and houses the Town Hall clock which every quarter hour sounds the old night watchman's call. The entire building is elaborately decorated inside and out and contains many sculptures and paintings of note.

Arrival of the Christmas Train
by
Johannes Achton Friis

1931

*T*he *Arrival of the Christmas Train* was painted by Johannes Achton Friis, the same artist who portrayed the arrival of the Christmas Boat on the 1917 plate. The custom of meeting the arrival of holiday trains and boats at Christmastime has been in effect in Denmark for a long time.

Shown on this plate is a group of happy Danes as they await the train filled with friends and relatives from distant parts of the country. It is about to pull into the station. The railway stations are always decorated for Christmas and even the trains reflect the season.

Denmark's first railroad dates back to 1847 when the line from Copenhagen to Roskilde was inaugurated. It wasn't until 1862 that railways were introduced on Jutland. Now there is a dense network of more than 3700 miles of track, most of which is operated by the Danish State Railways (called DBS for Danske StatsBaner) and the rest by private companies in which the state or municipalities have a financial interest.

The network boasts of 284 stations and ample rolling stock that operates on electric and diesel power and even a few steam locomotives remain. The latter are used only for family tours and tourist attractions in the summertime. By any measure the modern Danish railroad network is highly developed.

Most of the bridges connecting Denmark's many islands carry both railway and highway traffic. But to cross the Great Belt, the wide arm of the North Sea which separates Zealand from the rest of Denmark, the trains must be put aboard ferries. However, this will no longer be necessary when the bridge now being built is completed in 1996.

91

Lifeboat at Work
by
H. Flügenring

1932

*S*ince Denmark is largely an insular country, with more than 5000 miles of coastline, the sea has ever played an important part in its history. The Vikings once ruled the seas as well as a large part of the known world.

A tranquil sea is shown on several Christmas plates, but this is the first to depict the power of the raging sea. This painting shows a typical lifeboat of Skagen, the northernmost Danish town, located at the very top of the Jutland peninsula.

The sea in this area is always rough because the waters of the Kattegat and those of the North Sea fight a never-ceasing battle. The rescue crews must always be ready to perform their life-saving mission.

When the artist painted this scene he was remembering an accident which happened August 5, 1930 not far from Skagen. The American boat *Chickasaw* collided with the Swedish steamer *Femern*. The forward section of the *Femern* was cut off and sank with four crewmen aboard. The rest of the ship was towed into the harbor at Frederikshavn.

Many lives have been saved through the gallant efforts of these lifeboat crews. They are usually called upon to perform their services when conditions are at their worst. Unfortunately, the lifeboat crews have not always succeeded in getting themselves safely back.

Skagen and Frederikshavn, a few miles to the south, are two of the country's more important commercial fishing centers. Many fishing boats operate out of these two towns to fish the Skagerrak, the Kattegat, the North Sea and even the Barents Sea. With present day international limits on the size of catches, the Danes are looking into fish farming in order to maintain their important seafood export industry.

The Korsør-Nyborg Ferry
by
H. Flügenring

1933

*T*hose in charge of the first Danish railways soon realized that the efficiency of this new means of transportation in Denmark would require the use of ferries to cross the Sounds and Belts that separate the various parts of their country.

The Danish State Railways opened the first ferry service between Fredericia and Strib in 1872. These ferries, carrying only a single track, were discontinued when the Little Belt Bridge from Funen to Jutland (shown on the 1935 plate) was opened to traffic in 1935.

The ferry service across the Great Belt began in 1883 with the boats running between Korsør and Nyborg. Double-tracked paddlewheelers were used at first but now a series of modern ferries, among the best in the world, are employed.

Pictured on this plate is the motor vessel *Zealand*, built in 1933 and used to transport trains, automobiles, cargo and passengers. During the Nazi occupation in World War II, the Germans blew up the *Zealand* in retaliation for sabotage done to German transport by the Danish underground (see story for the 1940 plate). After the war the vessel was repaired and returned to service.

Ferry service between Zealand and Funen across the Great Belt now is in two parts. The Nyborg-Korsør route is used largely for the transport of trains and freight, while automobiles are transported between nearby Knudshoven and Halsskov. The Great Belt is 70 miles long and about 20 miles wide. The ferry trip takes about an hour.

This ferry service will undoubtedly become much less used after the new bridge between Korsør and Nyborg is completed in 1996.

Church Bell in Tower
by
Hans F. I. Tjerne

1934

Christmas Eve is *the* big event of the year in Denmark. Beginning at noon the shops, restaurants and other business establishments start to close so that their employees may go home to prepare for the Christmas Eve activities.

At five o'clock church bells in town and country ring out to summon the people to worship. The artist, Immanuel Tjerne, depicts the old-fashioned way in which the bells were rung in most village churches.

The bell-ringer, as a rule, was someone hired to do the job, often a devoted church member who derived great pleasure from this task, particularly at this time of the year. Everyone makes a special effort to attend the impressive church service on Christmas Eve -- even those who seldom or never go to church at other times. The churches are always crowded for this service.

The Danes hope for a white Christmas, and generally have it. If it has not already snowed, it frequently seems to start as the church bells begin to ring.

The Christmas Eve service begins shortly after five o'clock. The church is always beautifully decorated with evergreens and lighted by many candles. The minister is dressed in a black robe with a big white Elizabethan ruff.

The service is opened by a layman, the choirdeacon, in full formal dress. The crowded congregation includes many children anxious for the festivities that will take place a little later in the evening.

In front of the chancel stand several Christmas trees, their branches loaded with lighted candles. A solemn Boy Scout in uniform walks around each tree all during the service to make sure it does not catch fire.

The Lillebelt *Bridge Connecting Funen with Jutland*
by
Ove Larsen

1935

*I*t is easy to understand why the motif for this Christmas plate was chosen, for the Danes are justifiably proud of the many bridges connecting their 500-island country. This bridge, the *Lillebelt* (Little Belt) Bridge, was opened to traffic in 1935.

The *Lillebelt* Bridge connects Middlefart on the island of Funen with Fredericia in Jutland. It is almost three-quarters of a mile long and stands 108 feet above the often turbulent waters of the Little Belt, the arm of the North Sea which separates Funen from Jutland.

Construction of the bridge took six years, required 15,000 tons of steel, over one million cubic feet of cement and cost 32-million Danish kroner, a sizeable sum for the depression-era economy. In addition to a roadway and a pedestrian lane, the bridge supports a double railroad track.

At its widest point the Little Belt is 18 miles across, but is narrowest at the bridge. The water at this point, however, is unusually deep with a very strong current. This Christmas plate shows a train crossing the bridge shortly after it was opened.

The main point of interest in Middlefart is the Folk Museum; a little to the south is Tybring Vig, a broad bay with underwater archaeology sites and a little to the north the nearly flat coast gives way to steep dramatic cliffs.

Fredericia, established about three centuries ago as a rampart by Frederik III, has seen much strife against Scandinavian and German armies. To this day, on every evening of July 5, the town celebrates its 1849 victory when the Danes routed their German besiegers. Frederik III also conferred a special constitution on the town, designating it an asylum for religious refugees and others. Until religious freedom was established in Denmark in 1820, Fredericia was the only place in the country where people could worship as they wished. There was a Jewish synagogue and French Huguenots brought with them a cigar-making trade, a few remnants of which still survive. Today it is an important railway junction.

Royal Guard Outside Amalienborg Castle
by
Ove Larsen

1936

Whenever the royal family is in town a small crowd gathers at noon around the bronze equestrian statue of Christian V (see 1914 plate) to observe the daily changing of the guard ceremony. To please the largest possible number of spectators, the Guard takes the longest route from the Royal Barracks to the palace at Amalienborg.

The Danish people seemingly never tire of the spectacle and take great delight in showing off the pageantry to their foreign visitors.

It is truly a picturesque sight! The corps, 36 young men picked from among the tallest in the military, is dressed in light blue trousers and dark blue coats glistening with polished buttons and crossed with breast straps. Wearing enormous black busbies they march briskly along to the music of a 31-piece band. On special days, such as holidays or the monarch's birthday, the Guard parades in full-dress scarlet uniforms.

When the procession reaches Amalienborg Court there is much saluting and flashing of officers' swords. The band then forms itself into a ring and gives a short concert under the monarch's windows. After the music the *Dannebrog*, the world's oldest national flag, is ceremoniously brought from the palace as the men in the crowd bare their heads. The band then leads the retiring Guard back to the barracks by a more direct route.

On the left of this plate and in the background can be seen Frederik's Church, also known as Marble Church. The internal diameter of the dome, 98 feet, is only a few feet less than that of St. Peter's in Rome. For lack of money, the church remained unfinished from 1770 to 1894 when it was completed at the expense of C. F. Tietgen, a wealthy banker.

Arrival of Christmas Guests
by
Ove Larsen

1937

*T*his intercity bus is bringing family and friends to the Christmas night party. It is easy to detect the warmth with which the guests are being welcomed. The starlit night and deep snow provide an impressive and peaceful setting that contributes to a joyous Christmas season.

The church in the background is but one of many in Denmark dating back to the Middle Ages when Catholicism was the predominant religion. After the Reformation these churches were taken over by the State and became Lutheran Churches. Many church relics from ancient times are preserved and cared for meticulously.

The country has good intercity bus service, owned and operated largely by the Danish State Railways. Introduced in 1932, travel by motor bus was still somewhat of a novelty when this plate was issued.

The first buses replaced some discontinued railway lines in southern Jutland. Later the service was extended to the more outlying areas. By acquiring bus lines paralleling railway lines, the railroads have been enabled to operate more economically by replacing inefficient trains with motor coaches.

Denmark is a small country with a very well integrated transport system utilizing trains, buses and bicycles. High though their standard of living is, only about 60 per cent of Danish families own an automobile. Cars are expensive in Denmark. Prior to World War II, cycling was merely the cheapest way to get around. In recent years, high petrol prices and concern for the environment have given a boost to this pollution-free transport which had earlier started to decline in favor of the car.

Cycling, which helps Danes express their commitment to the Green movement and to get closer to nature, is a way of life. Every Danish town has throngs of cyclists speeding along special lanes reserved for them (there are more than 3500 miles of such lanes) and woe to any motorist who intrudes.

For commutes to work, Danes cycle to special station parking areas where they leave their two wheelers for trains or buses. The same is true for longer trips, although sometimes the cycle goes along on special racks on the buses. Many of the buses on longer trips also have a hostess to assist passengers.

Lighting the Candles
by
Hans F. I. Tjerne

1938

*T*his is one of the most original of all the Danish Christmas plates. It shows the entire country lighted by candles thus wishing everyone a *Glaedelig Jul* (Happy Christmas).

In painting the six candles at the top of Jutland and Zealand, artist Immanuel Tjerne had in mind an old celebration that took place very early in the morning on December 13, which before our present calendar was considered the shortest day of the year. The day was sometimes known as "Little Yule" because it was widely regarded as the beginning of the Christmas season.

In Sweden, a young girl -- usually the prettiest in the household -- was dressed in a white robe with a red sash to impersonate the Lucia bride. The name is derived from Saint Lucia who, according to tradition, was martyred in Syracuse about AD 300. Her name was connected with *lux* (light) and St. Lucia's day was celebrated as a festival of lights.

On her head the Lucia bride wore a wire crown covered with whortleberry twigs in which several candles were fastened. At first cockcrow, between 1 and 4 a.m., the candles were lighted and the Lucia bride went through the house awakening all those who were sleeping. She served them a sweet drink or a cup of coffee and sang a special song. Everyone called her *Lussi* (Lucia bride).

The custom, with some changes, has now been adopted in Denmark. However, it is celebrated only in the schools and in hospitals. Young girls dressed in white and wearing their crown of lighted candles visit hospitals to sing carols and hymns to the patients.

Ole Lock-Eye, the Sandman
by
Hans F. I. Tjerne

1939

*F*or more than 150 years Hans Christian Andersen's charming fairy tales have been delighting young and old alike while inspiring artists as in this Christmas plate.

The Andersen story of *Ole Lukoie* (Ole Lock-Eye) was first published in 1842. Ole Lock-Eye is an imaginary character, a dream elf, a Scandinavian Sandman, who comes around each night to make children sleepy.

He comes in very quietly for he walks in his socks. He sprinkles a tiny bit of sand in the eyes of children to keep them closed so he will not be seen. Then he tiptoes behind them and breathes softly on their necks to make them sleepier. He wants them to go to sleep so he can tell them stories; he knows more stories than anyone else on earth and he loves to tell them.

Ole Lock-Eye is always handsomely dressed in a coat of silk, but it is impossible to describe it because it is always changing color as he moves about the room. Under one arm he carries a plain umbrella and under the other, umbrellas with pictures on them. If the child has been good all day Ole holds an umbrella with pictures over the bed and the child is transported into a land of fantastic dreams. If the child has been naughty, Ole holds up the plain umbrella and the child sleeps restlessly and does not dream at all.

In Hans Christian Andersen's story, Ole Lock-Eye comes every evening for a week to visit a little boy named Hjalmer. Each night, Monday through Sunday, he takes Hjalmer on a series of exciting adventures.

On this Christmas plate Ole Lock-Eye is shown holding the umbrella with pictures over an evidently well-behaved child. The Christmas tree in the corner denotes the season and gives a hint of the sort of wonderful dreams the child is having.

Delivering Christmas Letters
by
Ove Larsen

1940

*A*lthough Denmark was at peace when this Christmas plate was designed, World War II was already in progress. Perhaps the artist had intended to symbolize the mailing of Christmas greetings but in view of the coming of the war, as loved ones left home to face danger, the postman was met each day in hopes he would have a letter from a dear one.

Danish postmen wear bright red coats that lend a splash of color to city streets even on the greyest days. Letter boxes are all painted red and on each is painted a coach horn, used on old stagecoaches, the symbol of the postal service.

Denmark retained her neutrality in World War I and hoped to do the same in World War II. Although Hitler had signed a non-aggression treaty with the Danes, German troops marched into Copenhagen in April, 1940 and within hours the country was in a state of occupation.

The government was forced to concede to German demands to secure their agreement to respect Danish rule. But the German demand for ever-increasing concessions led to an organized Resistance movement. At the end of August 1943 German demands reached the point that Danish authorities could no longer accede to them. The German military took over executive power and the Danish government and monarchy ceased to function.

From that time the underground Freedom Council directed the struggle against the Nazis. Acts of sabotage against railways and factories working for the Germans reached into the thousands with major operations against German military installations, depots, ports and ships as well. It published and circulated 235-million copies of illegal newspapers.

Reprisals were brutal with thousands sent to concentration camps or summarily executed. When the Nazis moved to implement the Holocaust, the entire country -- including King Christian X -- rose up to protect Denmark's Jewish population of 7000 with the result that only 200 were arrested by the Germans.

As the war went on the Resistance was able to play a major role, including disrupting movement of German troops from Norway to France. By the end of the war, when liberating British troops entered Denmark on May 5, 1945, the country was a full-fledged partner of the victorious Allied powers.

Horses Enjoying Christmas Meal in Stable
by
Ove Larsen

1941

*T*hese horses are enjoying the double rations that Scandinavians customarily give to all farm animals and household pets at Christmastime. The birds, ever watchful, are hoping for a chance to grab a morsel for themselves.

These horses are of the Oldenburg breed of workhorse. Denmark's other common types of draft horses included the heavy Jutland and Belgian breeds and the light Frederiksborg. The Norwegian pony was also common on the very small farms.

The number of horses in Denmark has decreased as agriculture has become more and more mechanized. The tractor has just about replaced the working horse except for those kept for pleasure or for historic preservation reasons.

Horse shows were popular events throughout the country. A favorite one was the annual country fair at the Bellahøj in the northern part of Copenhagen, discontinued some years ago. Here farmers would show their best cattle and horses, competing for prizes.

There are also many fine race horses in Denmark. Horse racing here dates back to the latter part of the eighteenth century. The Danish Derby, earliest of the Scandinavian derby races, was inaugurated in 1875, the same year our own Kentucky Derby began.

The country's major race track is *Galopbanen* in the Klampenborg Woods (see stories for 1905 and 1923 plates). Betting is government controlled and bookmaking is illegal.

Danish Farm on Christmas Night
by
Ove Larsen

1942

*T*his snow-covered farmyard scene is typical of the Danish rural homestead half a century or more ago. The comfortable steep-roofed house is warm and snug against the coldest winds, but the outdoor water pump is hand operated to fill the drinking trough for the animals, a cold but essential daily chore.

Denmark has always been an agricultural country. The climate is favorable and the soil is easy to till, though not particularly fertile. The Danes have long known the value of using fertilizer and import many tons each year.

During the German occupation in World War II Danish farmers were unable to get fertilizer, causing production per acre to drop considerably. It was also impossible to import the fodder and grain needed to feed the cows, hogs and chickens and most herds and flocks were reduced for lack of feed.

After the war it took several years for the farmers to get the soil back into condition, the livestock population rebuilt and farm machinery repaired or replaced. Today Denmark is one of the leading exporters of agricultural products, chiefly to Great Britain, in the European Economic Community.

Among the interesting crops grown in Denmark are giant beetroots, used as cattle feed, and a variety of cabbage with long leaves rather than the more familiar compact head. The typical small farm will be planted half to cereal grains, four percent for the fodder beets and with 20 percent left to grassland.

The Danish farmer always tries to increase his production whether it be bushels of wheat per acre or pounds of butter per cow.

Denmark had nearly 200,000 farms in the 1960s but by the 1980s the number had shrunk to 80,000 with a further decline being experienced in 1990s. Danish farms are small, only 5 per cent are 245 acres or more.

JULE·AFTEN·1943

The Ribe Cathedral
by
Ove Larsen

1943

*T*he oldest cathedral in Denmark and possibly in all Scandinavia is located in Ribe in South Jutland, Denmark's oldest town.

The monk Ansgar, who brought Christianity to Denmark and the North, in 850 built a wooden church on the site where the Ribe Domkirke (Cathedral) now stands. The Cathedral, dating back to 1150, was built of stone brought to this rockless village by ship from the Rhine River.

A 234-step red brick tower was added in the 13th century as a stronghold and lookout. It served to alert the low-lying community by the tolling of its church bell when the sea was about to flood the area. Once the chief port in western Denmark, Ribe is now four miles inland because the sea receded and silt filled the harbor.

Ribe began as a Viking settlement and was of great importance in the Middle Ages. Its days of glory ended when economic and political power moved to Copenhagen in the 1600s. Disaster befell it in 1864 when southern Jutland was lost to Prussia after the heroic battle of Dybbøl, becoming part of Schleswig-Holstein. The area did not return to Denmark until 1920 after an overwhelming favorable vote in a North Schleswig plebiscite.

The small houses, inns and courtyards of Ribe are much as they were hundreds of years ago. Set among the winding cobbled streets, the houses often have sagging roofs and windows askew to give the town an undeniable charm. The reassuring sounds of the night watchman are still heard. More than 500 buildings are included in a municipal preservation project, the largest in Scandinavia.

Church bells that once rang out four times a day calling people to pray have been replaced by a melody played by the church at 8 a.m., 12 noon, 3 p.m. and 6 p.m.

Annual summer visitors to Ribe are its storks. According to legend good fortune will come to any house where storks nest. For this reason the townspeople vie with one another in trying to attract the birds by erecting wooden foundations or nesting baskets on their roofs. The storks winter in Africa and, unfortunately, the number returning north for the summer diminishes every year.

The Sorgenfri *Castle*
by
Ove Larsen

1944

*T*his Christmas plate has been aptly called a "protest in porcelain" against the Nazi invaders.

When the Germans occupied Denmark in April, 1940 they imposed certain conditions on the government in exchange for permitting it to continue. But in August, 1943 these conditions became unbearable and government leaders refused to cooperate any longer. In retaliation the Germans confined King Christian X for a time to the *Sorgenfri* (Carefree) Castle in Lyngby, just outside Copenhagen.

In 1943, as the King sat near a window, a German soldier fired at him. The bullet missed but the windowpane through which it passed has been kept as a reminder and can be seen to this day in the Rosenborg Castle collection.

Although Denmark has one of the oldest democratic traditions in Europe, the great love and respect the Danish people had for Christian X is manifested by this plate.

The *Sorgenfri* Castle, pictured on this plate, was built in 1705 by Fr. Dieussart for Count Ahlefeldt. In 1734 it was enlarged by the famous architect, Thura, as a summer residence for Frederik V, then crown prince. It was here that Frederik IX was born in 1899.

Christian X, grandfather of the present queen, Margrethe II, was the monarch during the harsh years of the German occupation between 1940 and 1945. Despite the difficulties he managed to daily ride around the city on horseback, an important symbol of liberty for the people. In proud contempt of German regulations that Danish Jews wear a yellow Star of David as a mark of identification, the King wore the star on his own sleeve during those rides, inspiring a great many Danes to do the same.

Close to the *Sorgenfri* Castle is the extremely interesting *Frilandsmuseet*, an open air museum started in 1900 by Bernhard Olsen. Olsen wished to create for the enjoyment and education of the Danish people and their posterity a park where examples of typical Danish architecture could be preserved.

The museum continues to grow as farmhouses and various types of buildings are acquired and transported to Lyngby. There they are placed in settings typical of the region of Denmark from which they came. Every building is authentically furnished.

The Old Water Mill
by
Ove Larsen

1945

*T*he picturesque manner in which the old romantic water mills always seem to blend with the landscape has long inspired artists and poets. The water mill shown here is typical of those found in Denmark.

Formerly many such mills provided an economical means of grinding grain. The water mill superseded the old method of crushing grain by pounding it in a stone or wooden bowl.

These mills were built over a stream or beside it at a spot where an appreciable amount of falling water could be obtained by damming to create a millrace. One way of obtaining power from the water is to have a large vertically-mounted wheel with buckets on its rim which fill with water on one side, causing it to rotate. Another way is to use a wheel mounted horizontally or vertically with paddles extending into a swiftly-moving flow of water.

In either case a shaft, usually made of wood and extending from the wheel into the mill, drives a large millstone against a similar stationary one in which grain is fed through a hole in the center. The rubbing action of the two millstones against each other grinds the grain into meal or flour.

Today only a relatively few such mills have been preserved in the United States. They have been almost entirely replaced by hammer mills and the large modern flour mills that can blend several types of grain in the correct proportions to produce the many types of bread, cake and pastry mixes now available.

Some people, though, still believe that grain ground by the old water mills makes bread that tastes better and is more nutritious than bread made of flour from today's highly developed mills.

Commemoration Cross in Honor of Danish Sailors
Who Lost Their Lives During World War II
by
Margrethe Hyldahl

1946

*I*mmediately upon invading Denmark in 1940, the German occupation officials commanded Danish shipowners to order their vessels to the nearest neutral port. Most of the captains, realizing the shipowners were under duress, instead proceeded at once for the nearest Allied port.

At the time about 750,000 tons of Danish shipping was on the high seas, scattered all over the globe. Within a few months almost 200 Danish ships and 5000 Danish seamen were sailing for the Allied cause and as Britain's wartime foreign minister put it were "sharing all the perils of the war at sea."

Most of the Danish ships headed for Britain, greatly aiding that embattled country's ability to fight by providing needed additional shipping tonnage. In the beginning these ships sailed under the British flag but the Danish seamen, anxious to sail under their own flag, were permitted to fly the *Dannebrog*, the world's oldest national flag, starting on New Year's Day 1943.

Permission also was granted for the Danish flag to be flown on four British minesweepers manned entirely by Danish sailors. On the historic morning of June 6, 1944, when the Allied forces crossed the English Channel to storm the beaches of Normandy, more than a few ships were flying the Danish flag.

Of the 5000 Danish sailors who fought with the Allies, 1400 lost their lives. In one of the main squares of Copenhagen, overlooking one of the city's harbor canals, a simple but beautiful oak cross was erected in memory of those men who gave their lives fighting for the freedom of their country and of the democratic world. On August 29, 1951 the cross was replaced by an iron anchor.

JULE·AFTEN·1947

The Dybbøl Mill
by
Margrethe Hyldahl

1947

Only where Jutland joins Germany does Danish soil touch that of another nation. This area, populated by Germans and Danes, has for more than 150 years presented problems and frictions.

From ancient times the two provinces of Schleswig and Holstein belonged to Denmark, but Holstein was also considered a member of the German Confederation. In 1848 a war was fought to determine their sovereignty. The Danes were victorious, but the victory was short-lived.

In 1864 Bismarck, in power in Prussia, persuaded Austria to join him in regaining the two provinces. As before, the battle was fought in the vicinity of Dybbøl Mill. The outnumbered Danes fought heroically against overwhelming odds but in the end 5000 Danes lay dead and Bismarck was victorious.

Denmark was forced to cede both provinces, losing a large amount of land and a million inhabitants, about 200,000 of whom were Danes living in Northern Schleswig. Prussia promised that a later plebiscite would determine the fate of this area, but this promise was never kept.

After World War I the terms of the Treaty of Versailles required that the long-promised plebiscite be held, and the area was divided into the three voting zones: Northern and Southern Schleswig and Holstein. Accordingly, in 1920 the vote was held and Northern Schleswig voted by a wide margin to return to Denmark. The other two zones elected to remain German.

The historic Dybbøl Mill near Sønderborg became a symbol of the unconquerable spirit of the Danish people. It has been destroyed and rebuilt several times. Now it is a national museum and the ground around it is considered to be sacred.

Watchman, *Sculpture of Town Hall of Copenhagen*
by
Margrethe Hyldahl

1948

*T*he present town hall of Copenhagen, the sixth in the city's long history, is a comparatively new building, designed by Martin Nyrop and built in 1892-1905.

The building is mammoth: 420 feet long and 233 feet wide. The attractive structure is made of red brick, along with some granite, limestone and terra cotta. Above the main entrance is a bronze relief of Bishop Absalon, founder of Copenhagen.

While the 1930 Christmas plate shows the front of the Town Hall, this plate depicts one of a row of figures along the roof representing watchmen who guarded the city in olden times. The watchman, who is blowing a lur, is holding a long-handled mace, a war weapon of the times.

The lur dates back about 3000 years as a Danish musical instrument and although seldom seen or heard in modern times it is the trademark used to identify Danish butter and other agricultural products.

Inside the Town Hall's foyer is the first world clock, a unique and precise astronomical timepiece, invented and built by Jens Olsen. It is so accurate it is expected to lose only four seconds in the next 300 years. Among its many features, this fantastic clock gives all the time zones, the position of the planets, eclipses of the moon, positions of the stars for the next 3000 years and the Gregorian calendar.

Besides containing local government offices, the Town Hall also houses the Town Museum, which traces the appearance and history of the city through the ages. Exhibits include signboards, parts of buildings, guild relics, clothes, paintings and engravings.

It also accommodates the grand 11,250-square-foot Assembly Hall which holds marble busts of architect Martin Nyrop, sculptor Bertel Thorvaldsen (see story for 1952 plate) and storyteller Hans Christian Andersen (see story for 1954 plate).

Much of Copenhagen and its surrounding countryside can be seen from the building's imposing 346-foot tower, the tallest in the city.

Landsoldaten, *Danish Soldier from the 19th Century*
by
Margrethe Hyldahl

1949

*T*he Danish word *Landsoldaten* was used during the last century in the same way as the modern expression "G. I." is used in the United States. Both terms refer to the enlisted soldier.

The statue honoring the common soldier painted on this plate stands in the town of Fredericia in Jutland. It was erected in memory of those who fought in the 1848-1850 war against Germany (see story for 1947 plate).

The statue was created by the well-known sculptor Herman Vilhelm Bissen (1798-1868), a talented artist and student of the great Bertel Thorvaldsen (see story for 1952 plate). Bissen was awarded the Gold Medal of the Royal Academy of Art in Copenhagen after assisting Thorvaldsen in Rome.

Among his more famous works in Copenhagen are the statue of King Frederik VI in the Frederiksborg Gardens, the Frederik VII equestrian statue in front of the Christiansborg Palace and the statue of Moses in front of the Church of our Lady. He also created the statue of Johann Gutenberg in Mainz.

The town of Fredericia contains a number of other national memorials from past wars with Germany. The town was built in 1650 by King Frederik III as a principal fortress in Jutland and to secure communications between the peninsula and the island. Fredericia was given certain privileges which included religious liberty and right of asylum. Many descendants of French Huguenots still live in the area.

Not until after 1909, when the fortress was closed down, were buildings allowed outside the ramparts. Since then the town has developed into an important industrial center and railway junction. The inner town, though, still has a network of streets with right angle turns and high ramparts.

Kronborg Castle at Elsinore
by
Margrethe Hyldahl

1950

*I*n 1430 Erik of Pomerania, then king of Denmark, decided to impose taxes on all vessels entering or leaving the Baltic through Øre Sound. In order to enforce payment of these "Sound Dues," he built a fortress castle called *Krogen* at Helsingør (Elsinore)on the narrowest part of the Sound, only one mile across the water from Sweden.

The method of assessing taxes was both simple and effective. The captain of each vessel was forced to submit a list of all cargo and its value. It was not likely that the captain would be tempted to underestimate the value of his ship's goods because it was the king's prerogative to purchase the whole, or any part, of the cargo at the value declared by the captain.

For the next 400 years or more, these "dues" were an important part of Denmark's national income. They were abolished in 1857 when the nations using Øre Sound agreed to pay Denmark a total of 26-million dollars. The silver coins in the coffers of the customs house at that time were cast into silver lions which to this very day guard the Knight's Hall of Rosenborg Castle.

Between 1574 and 1584 Frederik II built Kronborg Castle, destined to become one of the world's most famous castles, where *Krogen* had stood. Originally built of brick, the castle was later encased in sandstone. It was partially destroyed by fire in 1629 and again suffered damage from Swedish bombardment in 1658. Rebuilt a number of times, the castle contains a statue of Holger Danske, a Viking chief whose bravery is said to inspire Danes in times of danger.

Shakespeare immortalized this castle when he chose it as the setting for Hamlet's Elsinore castle. It provides a fabulous stage for the many productions of *Hamlet* that have been performed here.

Helsingør is one of Denmark's most historic towns. Hans Christian Andersen lived here for a while and described it as "one of the most beautiful spots in Denmark, close to the sound, which is one mile wide and looks like a blue stream swelling between Denmark and Sweden."

Jens Bang, *New Passenger Boat Running
Between Copenhagen and Aalborg
by
Margrethe Hyldahl*

1951

*T*he *Jens Bang*, a ferryboat running between Copenhagen and Aalborg in North Jutland, was named in honor of one of Denmark's great merchants. The ship was launched in 1950 and has a displacement of 3284 gross tons.

Jens Bang took out a trade license in Aalborg in 1605, and before his death in 1644 became one of the richest and most important merchants of his time. He owned many ships and traded with Norway, the Baltic countries, France, Germany and Spain.

One of the main tourist attractions in Aalborg is Jens Bang's palatial six-story *Stenhus* (stone house), often called the biggest and best preserved Renaissance house in Scandinavia. Built about 1624 to show off his wealth, it also showed off his vindictiveness. He took revenge on his rivals and enemies by caricaturing them in grotesque carvings on the front of his house. He showed his anger at being denied a position on the town council by carving a caricature of himself with his tongue stuck out on the side of his house facing the town hall.

During World War II the basement of the house was the clandestine meeting place of an resistance group calling itself the Churchill Club which was responsible for numerous underground activities aimed at combating the Germans. Now there is a wine bar, open to the public, in this basement.

A bustling, successful commercial town in the Middle Ages, Aalborg today is Denmark's fourth largest city. Still successful, its prime location on the south bank at the narrowest point of the Limfjord, helps make it the busy commercial center it remains.

A few miles south of Aalborg is the Rebild Park. Land for this park was purchased in 1911 by some Danish-Americans. Every year on July 4th tens of thousands of Danes and Danish-Americans gather here to celebrate America's Independence Day. The Stars and Stripes fly in this park on equal terms with the *Dannebrog*.

The park houses a Lincoln Memorial Cabin built of logs from each of the 48 mainland states. The log cabin contains mementos of Danish migration to the United States.

Old Copenhagen Canals at Wintertime with the
Thorvaldsen Museum in the Background
by
Børge Pramvig

1952

*D*enmark's greatest sculptor, Bertel Thorvaldsen, was born in Copenhagen in 1770. He learned the art of carving very early in life from his father, an Icelandic woodcarver. At the age of eleven he enrolled in the Copenhagen Art School where his outstanding talent was soon noted.

When Thorvaldsen was 26 he won a scholarship to Rome where he worked for the next 42 years. He became known as the greatest sculptor of his day and his clientele included kings and cardinals from most of the European countries.

When he was 68 the Danish government prevailed upon him to return to Copenhagen and make his native city his permanent home. He returned on September 17, 1838 to a gala welcome. Bands played, ships in the harbor were decorated with flags and flowers were showered on him from windows above as men vied for the privilege of pulling his carriage through the streets. All Denmark honored him as the nation's most distinguished citizen and continued to do so until his death in 1844.

Thorvaldsen willed the city of Copenhagen his sculptures, his art collection and his fortune. The Thorvaldsen Museum, built to house this outstanding collection, opened to the public in 1848. The great sculptor is buried in the courtyard at the center of the museum.

The museum is a simple building of yellow stucco. A unique external frieze depicts Thovaldsen's triumphal return to Copenhagen. Inside the museum can be found all of the great sculptor's works, either the originals or castings.

JULE·AFTER·1953

Boat of His Majesty, the King of Denmark,
in Greenland Waters
by
Kjeld Bonfils

1953

*T*his was the centennial year for the Bing and Grøndahl Company and an important year in the history of Greenland.

This Christmas plate commemorates the visit of King Frederik IX and Queen Ingrid to the territory, only the second time in history the Greenlanders had been so honored by their monarch. The royal yacht *Dannebrog* is shown in the icy waters of Davis Strait, just off the rocky coast.

When the royal yacht docked at Godthaab, Greenland's largest town and capital, the entire population, then 2700 people, turned out to give their traditional nine cheers.

The Constitution Act of 1953, besides other reforms, gave Greenland status as part of the Danish Realm, sharing equal rights with Denmark. Previously it had been considered a crown colony since 1721 when Hans Egede, a Danish missionary, established a colony at Godthaab.

The Constitution Act of 1953 also permitted Greenland to elect two members to sit with the other 177 in the *Folketing*, the Danish Parliament. In 1979 the island gained home rule with an elected assembly which now has 27 members and an autonomous government. In 1985 it received its own flag and now is a member of the Nordic Council. Population now is about 55,419 of whom about 13,000 live in the capital.

Other important provisions of the Constitution Act abolished the upper house of the Danish parliament and provided that a woman could inherit the throne, paving the way for Princess Margrethe to become Queen Margrethe II in January 1972.

Birthplace of Hans Christian Andersen
by
Børge Pramvig

1954

*T*his is the birthplace of Hans Christian Andersen, Denmark's great writer of fairy tales known and loved around the world. He was born in Odense on the island of Funen on April 2, 1805, the only child of a poor shoemaker and his wife.

During his early years the family lived and worked in one room. His father died when Hans was eleven and two years later his mother remarried, but the new husband had little interest in the boy. His mother wanted Hans to become a tailor, but the lad dreamed of becoming a famous actor.

At the age of 14 Hans went to Copenhagen to try his luck on the stage. For several years he tried as an actor and a singer, but without success. After much heartbreak he decided to try for a literary career.

Having had little formal education, he found it necessary to return to school for several years. But he wrote constantly -- poems, plays, novels, fairy tales and eventually an autobiography. Soon his writings were recognized at home and in many foreign lands. He traveled extensively throughout Europe and was friend to many of the great personalities of the day.

Although he remained a bachelor all of his 70 years, it was not of his own choosing. Andersen was known to have been in love with at least three women, the most famous of whom was the Swedish singer Jenny Lind, but none returned his love. He always thought of himself as a poet, dramatist and novelist but the world remembers Andersen as a spinner of fairy tales.

The Hans Christian Andersen birthplace was opened as a museum in 1908 and in 1930 was enlarged with additional buildings. In the museum are letters, manuscripts, pictures and personal belongings of the author. There is also a library of about 2500 editions of his works in about 45 different languages attesting to his ultimate popularity.

The Kalundborg Church
by
Kjeld Bonfils

1955

Kalundborg is a small town on the western coast of Zealand. The town has colorful streets, a picturesque market square, a railhead and a port open to navigation all year.

The unique brick church pictured on this plate is the town's main point of interest. As were many of the old Danish churches, Kalundborg Church was originally built to be used as a fortress as well as a place of worship. It was built in 1170 by Esbern Snare, twin brother of Bishop Absalon, founder of Copenhagen.

The church is constructed in the form of a Greek cross and is unique in that it has one rectangular and four octagonal towers surmounted by spires. There is an octagonal tower over each of the four wings. These are dedicated to Saints Anne, Gertrude, Catherine and Mary Magdalene.

The fifth and highest tower is rectangular and rises in the center of the cross. It was necessary to rebuild the center tower in 1871 after the original collapsed. This tower is dedicated to Our Lady.

Inside the church is a carved wooden reredos, an ornamental screen behind the altar, dating back to 1650 and a notable granite font. The churchyard is enclosed by an old brick wall.

The church stands on a hill and the five clustered towers pointing heavenward are quite impressive. One of the most picturesque views of this imposing structure is from the ferryboat that runs between Kalundborg and Aarhus in Jutland.

In the vicinity of the church are a number of medieval buildings including some of the oldest in the country. A little to the west of the church is a park containing the ruins of Kalundborg Castle.

139

Christmas in Copenhagen
by
Kjeld Bonfils

1956

Christmas time in Denmark is very much as it is in other lands.

It is a time for family festivity, for being good neighbors, for renewing friendships and for helping those less fortunate. There is always an excitement about the season, part of which is undoubtedly genuine and part of which has been brought about by the commercialization of the holiday.

This plate shows how the streets of Copenhagen have been decorated for the Christmas season with garlands, colored lights, bells and stars. All the shops decorate for the holiday season and each has its own Christmas tree. Always, too, there is the big tree in the Town Hall Square (shown on the 1930 plate), twinkling with a myriad of lights. Copenhagen is lovely to behold at this season of the year.

On the last two Sundays before Christmas, the shops in the main part of the city open at four o'clock in the afternoon. But long before they open the streets are teeming with people who come not only to shop but to greet friends. Even though the wind may be blowing and temperature quite low, the crowds move along at a pace that would suggest a warm summer evening.

Music of at least one live band fills the air adding to the festive spirit of the occasion. People fill the sidewalks and sometimes the streets as well, making it very difficult for the buses and and cars to move along.

A trip to the heart of Copenhagen on one of these last two Sunday afternoons before Christmas is definitely part of celebrating the Yule in Denmark's capital city.

Christmas Candles
by
Kjeld Bonfils

1957

*H*ans Christian Andersen, in his beloved tale *The Fir Tree*, tells how the tree is selected in the woods and then brought home where it is decorated with little nets, hearts and cones filled with sweets. There are also gilded apples and walnuts hanging from its branches, and garlands of tinsel, flags and candles. "Was I really born to such a glorious destiny?," the fir tree wondered.

The hearts and cones have been cut out of colored paper and pasted or woven together by the children of the family during cozy December evenings. No one seems to know why there must be cones and hearts on the tree except that there always have been.

The candles are real, never electric. This may sound dangerous to Americans who burn the electric lights on their trees for weeks before and after Christmas Day. But on the Danish Christmas tree the candles burn only on Christmas Eve, and are closely watched.

Although the Danish people seldom use candles in their windows at Christmas, they do use them generously in decorating. The Danes refer to them as "living light" as they flicker softly in bowls, often with fir cones or pussy willow around the base.

The people of Denmark do place lighted candles in their windows one night of the year. When the Danes learned of their liberation on May 4, 1945 almost every home hit upon the idea of putting a lighted candle in the window. At the time it was a spontaneous gesture, but since then it has become custom to place a lighted candle in the window on the evening of May 4th to show the world that the light of freedom is still burning brightly in Denmark.

Santa Claus
by
Kjeld Bonfils

1958

*I*t is not unusual for a member of the family, or a family friend, to dress up as Santa Claus or his more traditional Danish counterpart, *Jule-nissen* (see story for 1959 plate).

This plate shows a little girl answering a knock on the family's door on Christmas Eve to find Santa Claus with a bag of toys over one shoulder and the Danish flag over the other. Santa joins the family group and gives presents to all the children.

A quaint old custom was once practiced by young people on New Year's Eve. Throughout the year each household saved its broken crockery and on the old year's last evening they smashed the cracked and broken dishes against the front doors of their favorite friends.

Then they ran, but not very far or very fast because it was part of the game that, if caught, they would be invited in for hot doughnuts. The person with the most broken crockery in front of his door on New Year's morning was, thus, the most beloved citizen in the community.

The Rønnebaek Church, located near Naestved in South Zealand, is shown in the right background of this plate. This is a typical village church from the Middle Ages and may have been consecrated to St. Benedict.

On the church door are four iron figures resembling horseshoes. The old people of the village tell a legend that the horseshoes belonged to a real horse that was once entombed under the porch. They claim that when a plague raged, a ghost-horse came running through the streets of Rønnebaek and the surrounding countryside shouting, "Get out! Get out!"

One farmer, placing himself in his doorway, cried to the ghost-horse, "Pass by my home, please!" This home is said to have been the only one spared by the plague.

Christmas Eve
by
Kjeld Bonfils

1959

*W*hile the 1958 Christmas plate shows Santa Claus, a later-day Christmas symbol who has gained a degree of popularity in Denmark in recent years, this plate depicts the Danish *Jule-nissen*, a popular Christmas character from olden times.

On this plate *Jule-nissen* is shown as he dances around the Christmas tree with the family on Christmas eve. He is similar to Santa Claus because he always brings gifts for everyone but is sort of like a leprechaun in that he is normally thought of as an elf. But this elf is supposed to be around the house all year keeping an eye on everyone and seeing to it that everything goes smoothly.

The *nissen*, it is believed, lives in the attic of the house but somehow remains invisible to the children. It is appropriate that the family cat appears on the plate because it and the *nissen* are good friends. Always on Christmas Eve the children place a bowl of rice and milk in the attic for the *nissen*. In the morning the bowl is licked clean, and the family cat is usually found purring contentedly in a corner of the attic.

Cats are now a popular pet in Denmark but their history here does not extend very far back. They were first introduced in the early part of the Middle Ages as presents from Oriental potentates with whom the Danes were trading. The prevalent type is the short-haired cat which originated from Persian ancestors. Siamese cats are also popular today as they make intelligent and sensitive pets.

The recorded history of cats goes back to Egypt about 2500 BC. There they were revered and often shown great honors. In the Roman Empire cats were protected by law and when one was sent abroad as a present it was given a name which was entered in a register.

Danish Village Church
by
Kjeld Bonfils

1960

Østerlars Church is one of seven round churches still found in Denmark. Located two miles from the village of Gudhjem, it is the largest and most interesting of the four round churches on the island of Bornholm, prodigious examples of medieval architecture.

Consecrated to St. Laurentius, its enormous support pillars attest to its ability to serve as a fortification, its secondary purpose. Stone steps inside lead to a second floor. Around the upper part of the church vault are various religious paintings dating back to 1230. They start with one of the Nativity Scene and end with one of the Last Judgment. In this latter scene the artist, in an effort to indicate ecclesiastical rank beyond question, used the size of his subject's stomach as a measure of his importance.

Dual purpose structures such as these churches, which were built in the mid-twelfth century, are rarely found outside of Denmark. There was obviously a definite plan behind the location of the four Bornholm churches as they are separated by approximately the same distance and all are situated inland creating a network of fortified structures. Impetus for the building of the round churches came primarily from the raids of Slavic Wend pirates. They saw plenty of service as fortresses right up to World War II.

Bornholm, with the best climate in Denmark, is a beautiful island in the center of the Baltic Sea between Poland and Sweden, two and one-half hours away by ferry; Copenhagen is 30 minutes by air. An important maritime center during the Iron Age, it became part of Denmark during the Viking era. It was occupied by the Swedes during one of their many wars with Denmark. But after the Swedish commandant was killed and the islanders drove off the invaders in 1660, by common consent they gave themselves to King Frederik III.

The last occupation came almost 300 years later when the Germans invaded in World War II. After liberation on May 4th, 1945 the German commandant refused to surrender. After warning the population, the Russians bombed the island and the Germans capitulated on May 9th.

The building shown to the left of the round church is the belfry, constructed several years after the church. The village of Gudhjem, which means literally "good home," is built on steep rocky slopes leading down to a harbor known for its herring catches. Bicycling downhill is prohibited there.

Winter Harmony
by
Kjeld Bonfils

1961

*A*n old nursery rhyme is supposed to have been the inspiration for the artist of this Christmas plate. Although the poet is unknown, it is believed that the poem originated in Sweden. It has been set to music and for a long time has been a Danish folk song. The words are:

Danish	English translation
Lille egern sad	*Tiny squirrel sat*
paa sin gren saa glad	*So happily on her bench*
pudsed' snuden sin	*Blowing her nose*
med sin lab saa fin,	*With her paw so fine*
dens smaa unger tre	*While her three little young ones*
havde ly og lae	*Found shelter*
i det store gamle fyrretrae.	*In the big old pine.*

The plate shows the red squirrel, the most common squirrel of Denmark, sitting on the branch of a pine tree nibbling on a pine cone. This squirrel has long red ears and is a different species from the red squirrel found in the United States.

Its Latin name is *sciurus vulgaris*. Although it is a beautiful animal it is being killed in some localities because it does great harm to trees and birds. It is hard to control this squirrel's population as it multiplies quite rapidly.

Early Scandinavians regarded the squirrel as the messenger of the gods, even carrying news to distant lands.

The building seen in the background is the white and red Kundby Church. It can be seen at a great distance as it is situated on a hill surrounded by open fields. Kundby is about seven miles west of the city of Holbaek on the island of Zealand.

Winter Night
by
Kjeld Bonfils

1962

Archaeologists have established that man has lived in Denmark for at least 6000 years and possibly for as long as 10,000 years. Recently signs of human activity were discovered in a pile of animal bones believed to be 80,000 years old.

It is also known that a highly developed "chieftain" culture existed in the area thousands of years ago. The many cairns found scattered throughout the country are ancient monuments marking the burial places of chieftains of various tribes. This plate illustrates a cairn at Mols in East Jutland.

The first signs of agriculture in this area date from about 2500 BC. Denmark, the warmest of the Scandinavian countries due to the influence of the Gulf Stream, probably supported the largest number of people in the early years. At any rate, there have been more archaeological discoveries made in Denmark, including an almost perfectly preserved body 2000 years old, than in the other northern countries.

During the Stone Age (3000-1800 BC) Denmark's abundance of flint and lack of metals resulted in a highly developed technique of flint-cutting. Many relics of the Bronze Age (1800-500 BC) show that the people were quite advanced in the making of bronze implements and ornaments. The Iron Age came next and extended to about AD 800 when the Viking Age commenced. It was probably during this period that the people started believing in the old Nordic gods such as Odin, Thor and Freya.

One of the two famous Jelling Stones (runic stones found in East Jutland) was erected by Harald Bluetooth (940-985). On it is written that Bluetooth was "the Harald who won all Denmark and Norway and made Danes Christian." The inscription is an exaggeration, but Harald Bluetooth did start the nation towards Christianity. The stone bears in relief a picture of Christ on the Cross.

153

JULE·AFTEN·1963

The Christmas Elf
by
Henry Thelander

1963

*T*he ever-popular Danish Christmas elf *Jule-nissen* is imaginatively portrayed on this plate as he exists in the minds of the children. Although *Jule-nissen* lives in the farmhouse invisibly, the children know he is always somewhere near, dressed in gray except for his gay red nightcap.

All during the year *Jule-nissen* takes a special interest in the livestock and household pets. He keeps them quiet and sees that they are fed and bedded properly. He also looks after the welfare of the family and brings gifts to the children at Christmas.

Jacob Riis, the Danish-American who was one of the first important social workers in America and whom Theodore Roosevelt once declared "The most useful citizen of the United States in his time," told about his childhood days in Denmark in his book *The Old Town*. When writing about *Jule-nissen*, he related:

When I was a boy we never sat down to our Christmas Eve dinner until a bowl of rice and milk had been taken up to the attic, where he lived with the martin and its young, and kept an eye on the house -- saw that everything ran smoothly. I never met him myself, but I know that the house cat must have done so. No doubt they were well acquainted; for when in the morning I went in for the bowl, there it was, quite dry and licked clean, and the cat purring in the corner. So, being there all night, she must have seen and likely talked with him.

This plate shows a farmer's wife bringing to *Jule-nissen* and his friend, the cat, a generous serving of *risengrod* (rice pudding) to which probably has been added an extra lump of butter. It is believed that the family can be assured true Christmas happiness only after the Yule treat has been placed in the attic for the little elf.

JULE·AFTEN·1964

The Fir Tree and the Hare
by
Henry Thelander

1964

*H*ans Christian Andersen's story entitled *The Fir Tree* provides the inspiration for the enchanting scene on this Christmas plate.

The little fir tree was quite unhappy because of its small size. It looked with envy at the tall, majestic trees nearby. For two winters the hare was able to jump right over the top of the little tree. The third winter, though, the fir had grown so tall that the hare was forced to hop around it.

Yet the tree was not happy for long. It wanted to be chosen by the woodsmen who came each year to cut down the tallest and straightest trees to be used as masts on stately ships that sailed the seven seas. How the little fir longed for such an adventurous life!

Near Christmas time each year other men came into the woods looking for the more shapely of the smaller trees. The sparrow told the fir that these trees were taken to the city and elaborately decorated. The little tree thought this, too, might be an exciting adventure.

Finally there came a Christmas when the little tree was the first to be felled. Soon thereafter it found itself standing in the center of a large room, surrounded by happy people, and decorated so magnificently that it trembled at the thought of so much splendor. The tree felt that this truly would be a glorious life but, alas, the next day it was stripped of its decorations and taken to the attic.

In the early spring it was dragged down the stairs. "Now," thought the little fir, "surely I shall see my old friends again -- the birds, the hare, the other trees and the sunshine!" Such was not to be its fate, however!

It was cut into small pieces and burned, making small crackling noises as the flames consumed it. These were really moans because, as Andersen said, "The tree knew that it was all over, and the story's over as well! All, all over! And that's the way of every story!"

Bringing Home the Christmas Tree
by
Henry Thelander

1965

*T*he place is Rebild Park in Rold Woods. The time is the Sunday before Christmas and the forest is a shimmering wonderland of snow. A watchful doe and her fawn stand immobile as a happy but weary family passes near them.

This family has been in search of the most beautiful tree of all, to be used as a Christmas tree. It is now late in the day and they are going home, dragging their freshly-cut tree over the snow. A Christmas-like star twinkles brightly overhead smiling down on the tranquil scene.

The trees that may be felled in this forest are marked in advance. Each year on the Sunday before Christmas families are permitted to choose and cut down their own *Jule* trees, paying for them as they leave the park. The excursion into the forest to select a tree is often one of the highlights of the Christmas season.

It rightfully is said that Rebild Park is unique among international monuments to peace. It is the only park in the world that has been established specifically to celebrate the American Independence Day, July 4th. (See story for 1951 plate.)

The park, originally 200 acres but now covering 425 acres of rolling hills, is always open to the public. On the Fourth of July both the American and Danish flags fly from every hilltop. The 50 state flags of the United States also are displayed.

Tens of thousands of Danish-Americans rendezvous here on this special day. Many come for the entire day to enjoy the rustic beauty of the park as well as the program, which usually includes speeches by prominent Danish and American citizens.

Home for Christmas
by
Henry Thelander

1966

*F*or untold centuries Danish fishermen have braved the North Sea for a livelihood. Often referred to as the "Mariners' Graveyard," there are few bodies of water among those sailed extensively that are rougher than the North Sea.

Because of its relatively shallow depth, steep and confused waves can develop in a very short time. Equally feared is fog which can develop suddenly and frequently. Nowadays most ships, even the smallest, are equipped with radio and fishermen get weather reports regularly. At the first mention of a possible gale, preparations are made promptly to seek the nearest harbor.

Although many of today's fishing boats are very large and capable of staying out weeks at a time, the ones shown on this plate are of an earlier, smaller type, many of which are still in use, usually handled by two to four men. On the bow of each boat are two letters, which identify the port from which it hails, and several numbers which have been assigned to that particular vessel.

On this plate the boats are coming home to one of the harbors on the west side of Jutland, the peninsular region of Denmark. It is Christmas Eve and each boat has followed the old Danish custom of attaching a small spruce tree to its masthead.

Quite probably the fishermen are returning early so they may go with their families to the traditional Christmas Eve church service. The boat lights have been turned on as the days are quite short this time of the year, particularly in northern Jutland.

It is obvious, too, that the sea has been rough as they made their way homeward, for the stabilizing sails have been hoisted.

As they enter the harbor, however, the men likely are thinking not of the rough sea behind them, but of the forthcoming holiday festivities with their loved ones.

Sharing the Joy of Christmas
by
Henry Thelander

1967

On this year's plate, artist Henry Thelander again has exemplified the spirit of Christmas by portraying a little boy feeding the birds on Christmas Eve. Let's call the little lad Jens, a typical Danish name.

During the long evenings of the previous summer Jens helped his father build the bird feeder from native woods around their home. It was placed among the small fir trees in their garden where the family could enjoy watching the several varieties of birds common to the area.

The feeder has been in place for several months and the birds have learned that food can always be found there. Now it is Christmas Eve and a blanket of snow covers the countryside. But Jens, bundled up in his heavy coat, does not feel the cold as he gives a Christmas treat to the birds.

It is an old tradition in Denmark that the birds and domestic animals share the joy of Christmas by receiving special rations.

After feeding the birds, Jens will take a bowl of rice pudding, prepared by his mother, up to the attic and leave it there for *Jule-nissen*, the Danish Christmas elf. This is the Danish equivalent of the American custom of the child setting out a treat for Santa Claus on Christmas Eve.

Jens must not tarry as the hour is drawing near when he will go to church with his family to participate in the five o'clock Christmas Eve worship service. When they return home there will be the big Christmas dinner, then the dance around the Christmas tree and, last but not least, all the presents!

As he feeds the birds surely Jens is thinking that this is the best day of the whole year!

Christmas in Church
by
Henry Thelander

1968

*I*n Denmark all who possibly can stop working the day before Christmas until after New Year's Day. The normal salutation upon meeting friends during this season is, "May God bless your Christmas; may it last till Easter!"

The 1968 plate depicts a highlight of the Christmas season -- the five o'clock church service on Christmas Eve. The churches are beautifully decorated with evergreens and are lighted with dozens of candles.

As befits a maritime nation, a model of a sailing ship may be found hanging from the ceiling in many Danish churches. The sea always has played an important part in the lives of the Danish people.

Before Christianity spread to this area, the Vikings worshipped many gods, including Ran, their sea goddess. Sometimes they called the sea "the land of Ran." It was believed that Ran had a giant net with which she drew down to her domain those lost at sea. Before embarking on important voyages or on raids, the Vikings offered sacrifices, including human beings, to their gods.

Christianity came late, and slowly, to this northland as these people found it difficult to give up the gods they had believed in for centuries. Christianity came to Denmark in the form of a monk named Ansgar in 826, in the reign of Harald Klak. But it was actually another 134 years before Christianity gained a real foothold when Harald Bluetooth became the first Danish king to be baptised.

When it did, the people gave up belief in their old gods but many of the old customs survived. The sea still provided a livelihood for many people so it is not surprising that the early Christians started the custom of hanging ship models in their churches. They were expressing the hope that their new God would bless their ships and the men who sailed upon them.

Arrival of Christmas Guests
by
Henry Thelander

1969

*T*he Christmas Eve scene on this plate could take place today or it could have been drawn from a similar setting a century or more ago. The Danish people readily accept new ideas when progress is the result, but even then they like to hold on to what was good of the old traditions.

Portrayed on this plate is the hostess of a country home as she comes forward to greet her guests, relatives who have come by horse-drawn sleigh to share the Christmas Eve festivities.

The woman coming from the barn carrying two pails of milk, expectantly convoyed by the family cat, indicates that milking is finished for the day. Undoubtedly the other evening farm chores have been completed as well.

After the horse has been unhitched from the sleigh, taken to the barn and given his extra Christmas rations, the family and guests will walk the short distance to the village church that can be seen in the background. After the service all will return to the house to partake of the traditional Christmas Eve feast, which is followed by carol singing and the gift exchange.

The farmstead is of the half-timbered design, still seen in much of the Danish countryside. Under the snow there may be a thatched roof. Not only do the Danes believe such a roof to be picturesque, but many contend it is a better roof, providing more insulation than the tile type more commonly used today.

Today's costs, as well as the potential fire hazard, usually prohibit the use of thatched roofs in new construction. Many farmers and householders in smaller communities, though, continue to maintain the thatched roofs they have had for many years.

Pheasants in the Snow at Christmas
by
Henry Thelander

1970

*F*ortunate indeed is the Danish farm family which can look out the window on Christmas Eve and see a number of ring-necked pheasants such as the ones depicted on this plate.

The handsome cock pheasant in the foreground adds color to the white countryside with his brilliant plumage which often grows to a length of three feet. The hen pheasant is a mottled brown, and not nearly as colorful as her male counterpart.

A native of China, the ring-necked pheasant was introduced in Europe late in the 18th century. They spread quickly and today can be found in most of the northern countries. In Denmark they are considered a game bird and the annual hunting season is during the latter part of the year. The birds will try to hide from the hunter but when flushed can rise almost vertically at great speed. They can maintain this speed, however, only for short distances.

Pheasants eat seeds and tender plants as well as many injurious insects. In the wintertime when food is hard to find they sometimes can be seen sharing the fare of the farmer's chickens.

The ring-necked pheasant is one of America's favorite game birds. It was introduced here much later than in Europe. In 1881 Judge O. N. Denny, our consul general in Shanghai, China sent 30 of these birds to Oregon. Twenty-six survived and were released in the Willamette Valley where they multiplied rapidly.

In 1887 Rutherford Stuyvesant brought a number of pheasants from England to his New Jersey estate. Today their range includes virtually all of the northern United States and into the western parts of Canada.

Christmas at Home
by
Henry Thelander

1971

*T*he time is Christmas Eve. After attending the five o'clock church service, the family has returned home and partaken of the Christmas feast. Now is the time the children have eagerly awaited.

Mother holds the baby meanwhile playing the old Christmas songs on the piano. Father, daughter, grandmother and grandfather sing and dance around the gaily decorated Christmas tree. Peace, harmony and happiness obviously reign in this home on this holy night.

The family is singing old Danish Christmas song favorites. One hymn they always sing is *Silent Night (Stille Nat)*. *Merry Christmas, Lovely Christmas*, to the tune of *Holy Night*, is another favorite. Other favorite Christmas songs include *A Child Is Born in Bethlehem* and *A Christmas Tree With Its Decorations*. Still another song the Danes always sing translates roughly as *High From the Tree's Top*.

After the singing comes the gift exchange. In some homes *Jule-nissen*, the Danish Christmas elf, or Santa Claus joins the family circle and distributes the gifts.

Christmas in Denmark, as it is in all Christendom, is a time for bringing the family together. Here all the festivities take place on Christmas Eve. Christmas Day is normally spent more quietly, giving the adults an opportunity to relax and visit with each other, and the children a chance to play with their new toys.

Mother and father have spent long December evenings with the children making many of the ornaments for the tree. The typical Danish tree is decorated with real candles, lighted only on Christmas Eve, and is topped with a shining star.

Christmas in Greenland
by
Henry Thelander

1972

*I*t is Christmas Eve in a little village in Greenland. Darkness has fallen, but it is not necessarily late. Since the northern part of the island lies north of the Arctic Circle, there are periods when the sun does not rise above the horizon.

The Arctic night lasts about four months at Thule, where the U. S. Army Air Force established a base during World War II. The base is still there, now operated by the U. S. Air Force within NATO. But the night lasts only about six weeks at Disko Bay. Certainly in all of Greenland the nights are long around Christmas time.

Two of the villagers are returning home, hurrying because it is very cold and also because they want to get home before the Christmas fun begins. Perhaps they are returning from a larger settlement where they were able to load their sled with many things that will bring joy to the villagers during the holiday season. One can almost tell from posture of the sled dogs that they, too, are happy to see the village lights in the distance.

Greenland, the world's largest island, was acquired by Denmark in Viking times but before World War II was considered by most to be a far-off Arctic territory. During the war air bases were established there and airlines used the island as a refueling stop up to the advent of today's big jets.

The original population of Greenland was Eskimo, but since 1721 many Danes have settled there, introducing their customs to the island. Christmas in Greenland undoubtedly is very much like Christmas in Denmark, except for the isolation of the villages.

Most habitation on the 839,000-square mile island is along a narrow strip near the seacoast. Population is approaching 55,000 with the bulk of the people in and around Godthaab, the capital. (See also 1953 plate story.)

Attempts to retrieve a B-29 bomber which crash landed on Greenland during a 1947 reconnaissance mission are to be made in 1995. None the worse for its 47 year icy entombment, the plan is to replace engines, propellers and tires and fly it out.

173

Country Christmas
by
Henry Thelander

1973

*H*enry Thelander's theme for this plate will take many back to their childhood days when they went to a large country house on Christmas Eve for the yearly celebration with grandparents, aunts, uncles, cousins and other seldom seen members of the family. For the grownups it was an opportunity to catch up on the family news for the past year and for the children, a time of excitement and anticipation.

The half-timbered house pictured, a combination of wood and masonry, is typical of many Danish country homes. These structures are so well built and well cared for that it is difficult to tell whether they are a few years or a few hundred years old. In many cases several generations of a family have grown up in the same house. Homes built in Denmark seem to stand much longer than homes are generally expected to last in America. Banks formerly gave 60-year mortgages on homes, but today the maximum is normally 30 years.

The home on this plate is ablaze with light and undoubtedly is festively decorated inside. Even the fir tree in front of the house has been brightly lighted, indicating to the passers-by that this home is happy that Christmas Eve has come again.

Mother and daughter are already being greeted at the door while father and son follow through the gate with their arms full of Christmas gifts. All have eagerly awaited this special night of the year.

Young and old alike are pleased that there has been a recent snowfall. Snow always gives the countryside a more picturesque appearance and most will agree adds much to the enjoyment of the holiday season.

Christmas in the Village
by
Henry Thelander

1974

*I*t is Christmas Eve in a little Danish village.

Once again the time has come for the men to close the shops early, for the women to put aside preparations for the Christmas dinner and for the children to temporarily forget the gifts they hope to receive later in the evening.

Now is the long-awaited hour when all in the village, young and old alike, go together to the village church for the annual five o'clock Christmas Eve service. The evening is obviously cold as the pond in the foreground is frozen over except for a small spot.

A pair of graceful swans are also featured in the foreground of this plate. Artist Henry Thelander has chosen to portray the mute swan, one of Denmark's favorite waterfowl. Although usually silent, this swan can produce a twangy trumpeting note and will hiss or snort when annoyed. The legendary belief that this swan sings a beautiful song just before it dies is the origin of the expression "swan song."

The male swan, known as the cob, is a very large bird weighing up to 20 pounds or more and measuring as much as five feet from beak to tail. The pen (female) is a little smaller. The same pair generally stays together for life unless something happens to one.

The cob brings the materials from which the pen builds a huge nest. Both help incubate the three to ten large pale green eggs, the cob taking his turn mainly at night. The cygnets hatch in about five weeks and four months later are fully fledged. They usually remain with their parents through the winter but are chased away in the spring by the cob.

Now the national bird of Denmark, the graceful waterfowl adds much enjoyment to the long Danish winter for the household fortunate enough to have them nearby.

Christmas at the Old Water Mill
by
Henry Thelander

1975

*S*cattered throughout Denmark can be found many charming old water mills such as Kjelddals Mill in Jutland, the subject of this plate. This picturesque old mill was saved from extinction in 1966 by the Danish National Museum Mill Preservation Board.

At one time as many as 3000 water mills could be found in Denmark but now only about 50 are left. The history of water mills in Denmark goes back for many centuries. Quite a few were built during the reign of the Valdemar kings, who considered it wasteful to let the water run into the sea without utilizing its power for the grinding of grain.

Some of the water mills built in the Middle Ages were in all probability built by monks coming from England, most of which then was ruled by Denmark. This is indicated by such names as *Klostermølle* (Convent Mill) and *Munkemølle* (Friar's Mill).

Between the 17th and 19th centuries the millering trade became so monopolized that not only were small farmhouse mills outlawed, but even hand querns were not permitted. This monopoly lasted until 1862.

For his pay the miller was supposed to retain only one-eighth of the grain brought in, from which he in turn paid his dues to the Squire, the Crown or the Church. These dues were always paid on St. Martimas Day, the day set aside to honor the patron saint of the miller.

It seems that there may have been times when there was some doubt in the customers' minds as to the accuracy of the method used to measure the grain. There was also a rumor that perhaps the miller did not use all his grain to make flour. In any event there was an old saying that, "A miller is never so drunk that he forgets to take his full quota."

Christmas Welcome
by
Henry Thelander

1976

"*L*ook, Mother, Daddy is here," the little girl shouts to her mother as she runs to greet her father who has just arrived. Her father, like all Danish fishermen, has been hurrying home to join his family for the biggest celebration of the year -- Christmas.

The church in the background is typical of the many Danish village churches built in the Gothic style some 850 years ago. They were usually surrounded by half-timbered houses, a style which remains popular throughout the country to this day.

The scene on this plate represents one of the many fishing villages on the island of Zealand, also the location of Copenhagen, the country's capital and largest city.

The island of Zealand boasts quite an interesting origin. Legend has it that Gefion, the Nordic goddess of fecundity, married the Swedish King Gylfe. She bore him four sons and when they had all come of age, Gefion decided she wanted to settle in Denmark. She asked the King for a divorce and also some land on which to build a new home.

The King granted her the divorce and only as much land as her four sons could plow away in 24 hours. Gefion transformed her sons into bullocks, who plowed away from Sweden within the time limit what is now the island of Zealand. The legend has it that the land taken from Sweden left a gap now filled by Lake Vanern, which is approximately the same size and shape as Zealand.

This legend has been immortalized by the Danish sculptor Anders Bundgaard, who in 1918 created the imposing Gefion fountain at the approach to the park at *Langelinie* in Copenhagen. This fountain depicts the famous plowing scene with the four bullocks straining at the plow as Gefion, right arm raised with lash, urges them on to even greater effort.

Copenhagen Christmas
by
Henry Thelander

1977

Christmas night in star-lit Copenhagen! What a wonderful view to behold!

Jule-nissen, dressed as usual in gray with a red cap, looks out from the skylight of his attic home and sees the illuminated Christmas tree in an adjoining dwelling. The ever-popular Christmas elf knows that this is the night he will receive his customary Christmas treat, a bowl filled to the brim with rice pudding (*risengrod*) and milk. He'll share the enjoyment of it with his close pal, the family cat.

According to legend, *Jule-nissen* in return will whisper into the ear of Santa Claus the list of Christmas gifts desired by the children. As important, he will also assure the family's happiness for another year.

This scene is in the old downtown section of Copenhagen, dominated by its signature landmark, the Round Tower (*Rundetårn*). This lofty building, near the University, was constructed as an observatory in honor of Tycho Brahe, Denmark's world-famed astronomer. It also serves as a tower for the attached Trinity Church. Three-hundred years later, in 1942, a new Planetarium was opened in the tower.

Designed by architect Hans van Steenwinckel, Jr., the tower was built in 1637 - 1642 by Christian IV, the famous builder among Danish kings. This king was so interested in leaving behind him great buildings as monuments that he often strolled through the streets of Copenhagen carrying a ruler to check how well the masons and carpenters were conforming to the architectural plans.

The 36 meter (118 feet) high Round Tower is famous for its 209 meter (685 feet) winding brick staircase. In 1716, while on a state visit, Czar Peter the Great of Russia rode to the top of the tower on his horse followed by the Czarina Catherine in a horse-drawn cart. Both returned unhurt from their experience and were hailed by the admiring crowd for their daring.

Today walking up the winding staircase is a must for all visitors to the city. Their exertion is rewarded by a fantastic panoramic view of the more than 800-year-old capital of Denmark.

A Christmas Tale
by
Henry Thelander

1978

*T*he Christmas season always brings to young and old memories of past Christmases. Many can remember a scene such as this one, sitting at Grandmother's knee listening to her read aloud a favorite Christmas story.

On this plate, the grandmother could be reading *The Fir Tree* by Hans Christian Andersen, a story the Danes never cease to enjoy.

The scene portrayed is traditional in many lands. Only the decorations on the Christmas tree indicate that we are looking into a typical Danish home. The Danish people prefer to light their tree with real candles, but only on Christmas Eve and under careful watch. The rest of the decorations are handmade by the family. The cones and hearts have been part of the Danish Christmas tree ornaments for generations.

The idea of a Christmas tree, as we know it, originated in Germany during the early 17th century. Some credit Martin Luther with first having introduced it, but this has not been authenticated. By the mid-19th century its popularity was well established throughout Germany and had spread to many other lands, It was introduced in Denmark in 1811.

There are many legends regarding the origin of the Christmas tree. According to one, it all started on a certain stormy Christmas Eve when a poor family living in a forest had settled around a cheerful fire. They heard a knock at the door, and upon opening it, found a little child, very cold, hungry and exhausted.

He was welcomed into the household, warmed and fed. Little Hans insisted on giving up his own bed to the stranger. In the morning, the family was awakened by the singing of angels and they found their little guest had been transfigured into the Christ-child.

Before leaving, the Christ-child broke off a branch from a fir tree, set it in the earth, and said, "I have gladly received your gifts, and this is My gift to you. Henceforth this tree shall always bear its fruit at Christmas and you shall always have abundance."

White Christmas
by
Henry Thelander

1979

*E*ven though there were palm trees and no snow on that first Christmas in Bethlehem, people living in areas where snow falls in the winter have come to associate Christmas with snow and are generally disappointed when the two do not happen simultaneously.

In Denmark, as in America, a white Christmas is always hoped for and frequently becomes a reality.

Henry Thelander was remembering the Christmases of his childhood as he painted the scene on this year's plate. He has depicted a typical little Danish village of yesteryear, including some of the stores, the half-timbered houses and a couple of windmills in the distance. In the foreground is the *kjøbmand* or grocery store. Thelander has used the older spelling rather than the present Danish usage of *købmand*. Across the street is a bakery identified by its golden sign near the door.

As the baker's wife starts out to deliver a loaf of freshly baked bread to a nearby customer, two children admire the tree in the grocery store window. One of the villagers has just completed her last minute shopping for items needed for the Christmas feast, and she and her husband are heading home in their sleigh. As darkness is falling, he stands on a platform at the rear of the sleigh to get a better view of the road.

Although the artist has portrayed a deep snow, the Danish climate varies greatly. Because of the proximity of the Gulf Stream to some parts of Denmark, winters may be surprisingly mild but often cloudy and gray. Or the entire landscape may become completely covered with ice, making travel difficult.

Generally the temperature drops to freezing or below for about 100 frosty days during the winter season. Perhaps it is the long gray winter which makes the Danes so appreciative of the sunny days of summer.

Christmas in the Woods
by
Henry Thelander

1980

*I*t is Christmas Eve and night is falling. The small group of deer approaching the feeder seems to hesitate as if sensing that something is different. Someone with the holiday spirit has added the extra rations that all Danes feel their animals deserve at Christmas time.

If Henry Thelander had the "old days" in mind when he painted this scene, it could have been in one of several areas of Denmark, particularly in Jutland. Nowadays, though, most of the deer found in Denmark are in *Dyrehaven*, the deer park near Klampenborg. Here about 2000 of these timid, graceful creatures wander about without fear. A group of 100 or more can often be seen in the vicinity of the *Eremitage*, the royal hunting castle built by Christian VI in 1736.

Hunting in those days was the prerogative of the nobility. They would usually have hunts that lasted three days. On the first day all would gather at the coffee table at eight, dressed in hunting attire. After breakfast the sound of the horn would send them off in carriages designed to take the rough roads and open fields. Many beaters would be sent out in advance of the hunting party to drive the game towards the hunters.

Throughout the morning the hunters roamed the woods and fields. At noon-time they would meet at a designated place, usually a country cottage, where open-faced sandwiches and perhaps a hot dish would be served. In the evening a hearty dinner would be served, and afterwards there would be billiards and cards for those not too weary to participate.

On the third day the ladies arrived and dinner that night became a more elaborate affair. After dinner there would be music and dancing until the wee hours, and then a supper was served.

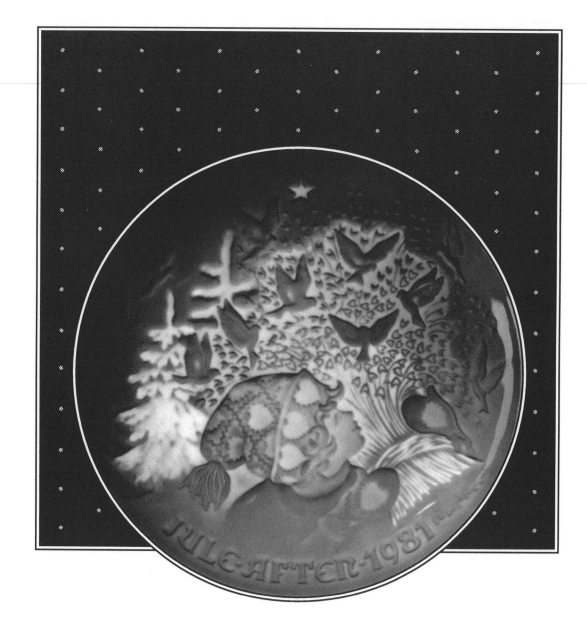

Christmas Peace
by
Henry Thelander

1981

*T*he Christmas season in Denmark is a happy and a busy time. It is the favorite festival of the year and most families delight in making elaborate preparations. The women prepare many special foods for the big Christmas feast.

The farmers make sure that there are extra rations for their animals. Perhaps this custom started with the legend that the animals which eat from the manger stand at midnight in honor of Christ's birth.

The birds are also remembered on the farm and in the city. In the rural areas sheaves of grain are tied to poles. Generally wheat is used as shown on this plate but sometimes it is a bundle of corn. In the cities boys and girls tie bunches of grain to porches and balconies; what the birds do not eat on Christmas Day is left for them to finish later.

An old Scandinavian custom still remembered by some of the old-timers, was the *jule-kasse* or the "Christmas Box." The *jule-kasse* was tossed inside by someone who knocked and jumped quickly out of sight when the door was opened. The present often was wrapped in a bundle of hay or straw or even a bag of chaff.

Sometimes it took a while to find the gift inside all the wrapping. In fact, it has been compared to "finding a needle in a haystack." Once the gift package was found it was sometimes necessary to unwrap one box after another, each one smaller than the last. The longer it took to find what the present was and who gave it, the more successful the *jule-kasse*.

The little girl on this year's plate is wearing her Christmas cap and mittens which are decorated with hearts, a favorite symbol of Christmas in Denmark. Seldom is there a Christmas tree without a few red and white hearts hanging from the branches. The little girl appears to be enjoying herself as she does her bit to make Christmas a happier time for the wild birds.

The Christmas Tree
by
Henry Thelander

1982

Christmas trees are often sold on street corners in the cities of modern Denmark, but it is still not uncommon for the people in small villages to go into the woods and cut down their own tree.

On this year's plate Henry Thelander portrays two children returning from the woods bringing home their Christmas tree. Darkness is falling and the older child has lit his lantern as he leads the way.

The tree selected, probably a spruce or a fir, was carefully chosen for form and size. It normally will be set up in the living room and long strings of small Danish flags entwined about it. Tinsel will be draped around the branches, various ornaments added and a star placed at the top. Around the base, of course, will be the presents.

Before the Christmas festivities start the home is thoroughly cleaned, and on the farm the process of tidying up extends to the barnyard and the stables. There is an old superstition to which some farmers still cling concerning farm implements left outside at Christmas time. It is believed bad luck will surely pursue such a careless farmer during the coming year.

The big celebration in Denmark is on Christmas Eve. Christmas Day is spent rather quietly at home or visiting relatives and friends. Merriment, however, continues between Christmas Day and New Year's Eve, which in Denmark is a night for pranksters similar to Halloween in the United States. A villager is not surprised to find his front gate hung on a flagpole and a farmer may wake to find some of his equipment perched on the barn roof.

Shortly after New Year's Day, though, the merrymaking is over, and the school holidays come to a close. The children go back to school and life, once again, becomes normal for the entire household.

Christmas in the Old Town
by
Edvard Jensen

1983

*B*ing & Grøndahl's new plate artist, Edvard Jensen, introduces his work to collectors with this year's plate, *Christmas in the Old Town*.

The scene may be one he remembers from his childhood. We are all prone to look back during the Christmas season, more than at any other time of year. It is at this time that we recollect many of the happenings of our youth, and even stories that go back beyond our own time. We remember our parents and grandparents telling how things were in their days. But one of the real joys of Christmas for many is remembering one's own childhood Christmases.

As a child the artist undoubtedly read the fairy tales of the great Danish storyteller, Hans Christian Andersen. He may have been remembering the much-loved one entitled *The Old Street Lamp* even though the lamp he portrays appears to be a gas lamp. Since the street lamp Andersen so lovingly wove his tale around was one using oil, it is doubtful that this is the one about which he wrote. The general design, however, is one that was used in Denmark for many generations.

In any event, the artist has depicted a cold and snowy Christmas Eve. Two hardy birds huddle near the lamp, trying to get a little of the warmth emanating from the light. Perhaps they have been fortunate enough to have found one of those Christmas meals the Danes put out for their feathered friends.

If so, they are now happy and content, and have settled down in a warmer spot to spend the night. They are oblivious to all the Christmas celebrations going on in homes around them.

The Christmas Letter
by
Edvard Jensen

1984

*I*t is Christmas time and even the children enjoy sending Christmas greetings to friends and relatives. Edvard Jensen's plate this year depicts a boy mailing a letter. As one looks at the plate it is easy to visualize some of the possible recipients.

Perhaps it is a note to his grandparents, or maybe a card to his favorite school friend, or it might even be a Christmas greeting to the little girl he met last summer while the family was on vacation. The boy may be mailing his letter to Santa. The postal service in Denmark always responds to such a letter by sending a little present to the child.

Certainly more mail is sent and received at Christmas time than at any other time of the year. During this season the mailman is eagerly awaited each day for he often brings greetings from old friends and far away relatives, some of whom are heard from only at this time of year.

It is a long-standing custom that mailboxes in Denmark are painted red. On each is shown a coach horn of the same type used for many years on the old stagecoaches. It is now a symbol of Scandinavian postal services.

The lad pictured on this year's plate is not quite tall enough to reach the mailbox but has solved this problem by standing on his sled. The fact that there are only a few footprints indicates the snow is freshly fallen.

The new snow has encouraged the child to get out his sled, always a prized possession. The Danish youngster regards his sled during the snow season with the same kind of pride and affection he holds for his bicycle during the rest of the year.

Now that the snow and holiday seasons have arrived, it is a wonderful time of the year. Snow is always wished for in Denmark at Christmas. Usually the weatherman obliges but it is never a certainty.

Christmas Eve at the Farmhouse
by
Edvard Jensen

1985

*N*ight has fallen on this Christmas Eve, and the usually quiet country home is ablaze with light. The Danes believe that a house brightly lighted at Christmas time extends a welcome to all, and they do a great deal of visiting during the holiday season.

Danish housewives bake for weeks in advance because everyone who comes must join the family in food and drink or else the visitor will bear the Christmas spirit away from the house. This would be a real tragedy because it could not be recaptured until the next year.

The cat is looking at the house from his domain in the barn and is wondering why this night seems so different. It may be that he has noticed the dish of rice porridge left in the barn for his friend *Jule-nissen*, the Christmas elf who lives in the barn or the attic and brings Christmas presents to the children. He also looks after the family's welfare all year.

The cat may have even noticed a small sheaf of grain on a pole in the gable of the barn, the family's traditional gift to the birds at Christmas although some children say it's for Santa's horse. Undoubtedly it is a custom that dates back to pre-Christian days as originally the sheaf was intended for the horse belonging to Odin, the chief Scandinavian god. Odin was usually depicted as a stately man with one eye which represented the one sun in the universe. He was wrapped in a blue mantle spangled with stars and rode a white horse named Sleipner.

This is the first year in the 91 years Bing & Grøndahl has made Christmas Plates that the artist has personally signed (in gold) each of the plates being distributed in the United States.

Silent Night, Holy Night
by
Edvard Jensen

1986

*T*his year Edvard Jensen features the gateway to the churchyard of one of the hundreds of old village churches found throughout Denmark. This particular one is located in Søllerød, a few miles north of Copenhagen. The church and the famous inn in this village were once part of a farm.

The open gate and the footprints in the snow indicate it is Christmas Eve and the annual five o'clock service has begun. The church is always beautifully decorated with evergreens and lighted by many candles. Although the Danish people as a whole are not great churchgoers, few miss this service as it heralds the arrival of the Christmas season.

After the church service all go home to a big Christmas dinner. This always starts with a big bowl of rice porridge, sprinkled with cinnamon and a piece of butter in the center. Somewhere in the bowl of porridge is an almond and he who finds it gets a special present. Somehow one of the younger children usually finds the almond. The porridge is followed by the roast goose stuffed with apples and prunes, usually served with red cabbage and caramel-browned potatoes. Dessert is often apple cake (layers of bread crumbs, applesauce and jam) topped with whipped cream.

After dinner the whole family joins hands and dances around the Christmas tree singing old Christmas favorites. Next comes the gift exchange and sometimes a visit from *Jule-nissen*. The children are allowed to stay up late on this special evening, but after the gift exchange they are tucked in for the night with their Christmas gifts stacked at the foot of the bed.

The Snowman's Christmas Eve
by
Edvard Jensen

1987

*D*arkness has fallen but enough light shines from the windows of the old half-timbered houses for the children to complete their task. For hours they have frolicked in the snow and have built a snowman they can be proud to show. Much happy laughter accompanied their labors and now and then the work lapsed into snowball battles with squeals of both joy and triumph.

Now, at last, they are tired and beginning to think of the warm Christmas festivities inside with their families. A final look at their snowman reveals just one small detail overlooked. The little girl points out that their friend will need a cap for this frosty night and she gleefully places her own upon his head.

The boys have been out looking for a little tree because even a snowman must have his own Christmas tree on Christmas Eve. They place the tree in the snowman's arms and all stand back to admire their creation before calling "Good Night" to him.

The snowman will stand proudly in the village street during this Holy Night in the clear light of the Star of Bethlehem. He seems to be smiling, perhaps a little wistfully, after the children have gone. He knows they will return tomorrow but he will no longer be the center of their attention. They will race off on new sleds or will be playing snugly indoors with dolls in lace and soft curls. He can never join the warm Christmas circle indoors but he knows he was one of the children's first Christmas delights.

The Danish people -- young and old alike -- love the winter outdoors. While the children were creating their snowman their older brothers, sisters and cousins might well have been skiing or ice-skating as both are favorite winter sports in Denmark.

Hans Christian Andersen in the King's Garden
by
Edvard Jensen

1988

*T*he place is *Kongens Have*, the King's Gardens, in which is Rosenborg Castle. The time is Christmas Eve and the birds are picking at bits of food left behind by the children who have been playing around the statue of Hans Christian Andersen.

The statue is one of several of this famous Danish story teller to be found throughout the country. His stories, translated into 45 languages, are well known throughout the world. Here Andersen is featured in a pose as if he is telling one of his much loved tales. All is quiet now as those who were in the garden only a short time ago are now at home celebrating Christmas Eve.

Rosenborg Castle, with its curved gables and sandstone ornaments on red brick walls, is an outstanding example of 17th century Danish architecture which was influenced by the Dutch Renaissance style. It was built between 1608-1617 by the great builder, Christian IV. When it was built the site was a little outside the city but now, due to the growth of Copenhagen, it is in the center of the city. Christian IV built it as a summer residence and it was used as such by the Danish kings for almost a century.

The castle is now a museum open to the public and is one of the great tourist attractions in Copenhagen. It is famous for housing *The Chronological Collections of the Danish Kings.* These collections include china, glass, furniture, paintings, et cetera, which have belonged to the Danish kings beginning with Christian I. Many of the rooms contain the original furnishings, including tapestries, furniture and portraits. The coronation robes and a breathtaking display of all the Danish crown jewels are also found in the castle.

All the Rosenborg collections still belong to the reigning monarch. Not only does the Queen make use of the jewels from time to time but also the furniture and porcelains are occasionally used by the Court.

Christmas Anchorage
by
Edvard Jensen

1989

Christmas peace descends upon the beautiful old sailing vessels tied up before the charming, restored residences along the Nyhavn Canal in the heart of Copenhagen, just east of *Kongens Nytorv*, the cultural center of the city. Pleasure craft by the hundreds line Copenhagen's many canals.

In the center of *Kongens Nytorv* (King's New Square) is a statue of Christian V. At the close of each school year students come in horse-drawn wagons to dance around it, celebrating the term's end.

The canal, built in 1671 - 1673, reaches from *Kongens Nytorv* to the water leading into Øre Sound, between Denmark and Sweden. The west end of the canal is the departure point for the hydrofoil to Malmö in Sweden, just across the sound from Copenhagen. Nearby, passenger ships depart for Norway and other points.

This part of the city has been referred to as the "Greenwich Village" section. Hans Christian Andersen, Denmark's great storyteller, moved into this section when he came to the city as a young man in 1845. He lived there for about 12 years.

At one time it was an area of ill repute where brawls were commonplace. Nowadays, however, it has been gentrified with the restoration of its 18th century houses and Copenhagen is justly proud of the area.

In 1728, and again in 1759, Copenhagen endured disastrous fires that destroyed most of the city but each time the houses in the Nyhavn area were spared. Copenhagen is reputed to have some 2000 restaurants; some of the finest can be found in Nyhavn. They have great views of the fleet of old-time sailing ships which dock along the canal.

At Christmas time the ships sport a small fir tree atop each mast. (By the way, the custom of placing a fir tree at the "topping out" of a building project also originated in Denmark.) Also in the canal is *FYRSKIB XVII*, a stout old lightship dating from 1893, permanently moored and serving as a floating museum.

Changing of the Guard at Fredensborg
by
Edvard Jensen

1990

Queen Margrethe and her family – husband Prince Henrik and their sons Prince Frederik, heir to the throne, and Prince Joakim -- spend much time in the spring and fall at Fredensborg Palace. The Royal Family sometimes spends the Christmas holidays here, too.

When they are in residence the Royal Guard is also stationed here and holds its famous changing of the guard ritual at noon each day. On this plate, however, the designer has taken artistic license to change the guard on Christmas Eve.

Now the peace and quiet of the elegant baroque palace is broken by the guards' band as it escorts the replacements to their posts, plays for the changing of the guard, and marches the men relieved from duty back to their warm and cozy quarters.

The men are members of the Royal Life Guards, established by King Frederik III in 1658 as his personal guard during Denmark's wars with Sweden. Several hundred years later they still perform the same service for the Danish Royal Family wherever they may be in residence.

Fredensborg Palace is located in the little town of the same name in North Zealand. It was built by Frederik IV in 1721 - 1723. After several alterations and enlargements it was given its present appearance by the Danish architect C. F. Harsdorff in 1774 - 1776.

The palace has 420 rooms grouped around Dome Hall. It is an exquisite setting for royal parties and houses some very valuable paintings. The surrounding park, which runs down to a lake, *Esrum Sø*, is one of the most beautiful in Europe. The Marble Garden, the Royal Family's private garden, contains many baroque Italian sculptures and an enchanting rose garden.

There are guided tours through the palace during the month of July when the Royal Family is usually in Copenhagen or at the Marselisborg Palace near Aarhus in Jutland.

The Copenhagen Stock Exchange at Christmas
by
Edvard Jensen

1991

*I*t is Christmas Eve and the beauty of the starlit night causes the pedestrians to pause as they cross the bridge near the old Stock Exchange.

This snow-covered building is known in Denmark as the Bourse. It is situated close to Christiansborg, home of the Danish Parliament, and faces one of Copenhagen's many canals. Richly decorated with sculptures, it is one of the finest examples of Renaissance architecture by Denmark's great builder, Christian IV.

The brothers Lorentz and Hans van Steenwinkel were commissioned to construct the Bourse in the immediate vicinity of the harbor. When completed in 1620, the king was unhappy with the architectural adornments and ordered dormers added to the front of the building. Over the roof, he added the tower with its distinctive green copper dragon spire. Tradition has it that Christian IV actually had a hand in the twisting of the tails of the four dragons which form the spire.

The building housed the Danish Stock Exchange until 1974, at which time the main part of the business was moved to another area. The red brick Bourse still remains the oldest stock exchange in the world still in use, at least in part, for its original purpose.

With its steep roof, tiny windows and gables, the building is indeed one of Copenhagen's greatest and the people are justly proud of it. This is evidenced by the fact it is shown on this year's plate as well as being depicted on the very first Christmas plate. The 1895 plate, *Beyond the Frozen Window*, showed the city's skyline and included the outline of this famous building.

The Pastor's Christmas
by
Jørgen Stensen

1992

*T*his peaceful Christmas scene is the site of the church and pastor's home at Nøddebo in North Zealand.

The church is very old, dating back to the 1100s, and was originally built as a pilgrimage church at the holy Magdalene Spring in the middle of Grib Forest. The spring is still welling up near the church as it has done since the church's founding. The interior of the church is adorned with Gothic frescoes by two artists, the "Master of the *Undløse*" and the so-called "Master of the Long Noses."

The present parsonage was built in the middle of the 1700s as a farmstead and was converted to a parsonage in 1910. Preserved in the parsonage today are the fine wainscots, doors and door frames from the long ago demolished royal castle of Hirscholm.

This year's plate shows the pastor and his young son returning home in their horse-drawn sleigh. They have been in the woods selecting the tree for this Christmas. Mother waves to them from the doorway as she watches their homecoming.

She is dressed warmly as though, perhaps, she has been outside looking for them since night is falling and the stars are already twinkling above. They have returned much later than anticipated because it took a long time to choose just the right tree; in their search they went farther and farther into the forest. It has been a trip, though, the pastor's son will always remember.

The boy will probably help make some of the ornaments for the tree and may get to help decorate it. On Christmas Eve, after the festive dinner and before the gift exchange, all the relatives will join hands and dance around the tree singing Christmas carols.

The tree is indeed a very important symbol of the season for every Danish home.

Father Christmas in Copenhagen
by
Jørgen Nielsen

1993

*S*troget, Copenhagen's answer to Fifth Avenue or Bond Street, is featured on this year's plate. Also known as the Walking Street, it is the main pedestrian shopping area in the heart of the city running eastward from *Raadhuspladsen* (City Hall Square). The main portion of *Stroget*, a series of streets too narrow for cars, is known as Frederiksberggade.

This pedestrian district has a rich history dating back to the 12th century when earthworks were built around what is now the city's administrative and political center. It is also the spot from which any other place in the nation measures its distance to the capital. Through the ages great fires have ravaged the city, but the soul of the Walking Street has survived.

Copenhagen is a mecca for shoppers in search of impeccable designs and top-notch quality. Nowhere else in the city can so many fine stores be found in one area as in *Stroget*. Most of the manufacturers of the fine products for which Denmark is famous, such as Bing & Grondahl, Holmegaard, Royal Copenhagen and Georg Jensen to name only a few, have stores here. Every tourist to Copenhagen considers a visit here a must.

Christmas is never quite complete for Copenhageners without a trip to *Stroget*. There they not only shop but enjoy seeing the beautiful Christmas decorations put up by the city and the stores. There, too, they expect to meet and chat with friends they have not seen for a long time.

It is during this season one can usually find Father Christmas, the European equivalent of Santa Claus, somewhere in the area. This year's motif depicts Father Christmas greeting two young children as they stroll the *Stroget* with their parents.

215

A Day at the Deer Park
by
Jørgen Nielsen

1994

*F*or the 100th plate in the unbroken succession of Bing & Grøndahl's famous series, artist Jørgen Nielsen has chosen to depict Christmas at one of Denmark's most outstanding parks.

Time passes slowly on Christmas Eve when you are a youngster awaiting presents after dinner. Mother has bundled up the children and sent them off to play for the day at Dyrehaven, the Deer Park, where time will seem to go faster.

The children will go sledding in the woods and ride their ponies near Peter Liep's House, now a fine old restaurant, pictured on this year's plate. The original structure was built in 1888 bearing the name *The Well House* but since then it has been destroyed by fire and rebuilt several times.

The park is located just ten kilometers north of Copenhagen and dates back to the 15th century. For hundreds of years it has been a favorite place of recreation for the Danes. In addition to horseback riding and sledding, skiing is a favorite winter sport in the park. In the summer they come here to enjoy carriage riding and family picnics.

This large park of about 2500 acres of woods serves as a sanctuary for fallow and red deer. Here are some of the most beautiful woods in all Denmark. Tall birches are the most numerous but oaks and fir trees are also found in great numbers. The deer have completely eaten away the undergrowth, giving this wooded area a character of its own. Here, too, is the charming old castle called *Eremitage* (The Hermitage) which was featured on the 1923 plate.

On the edge of Dyrehaven is Bakken, a good old-fashioned amusement park even older than the world-renowned Tivoli Park in Copenhagen. It is one of the largest amusement parks in northern Europe and the income from it is used for the upkeep of the forest and the deer.

Copenhagen - The City of Towers
by
Jørgen Nielsen

1995

*I*n 1895 Bing & Grøndahl created the first commercial Christmas plate entitled *Behind the Frozen Window*. This year, to commemorate the centenary of this plate, artist Jorgen Nielsen has re-created the famous frozen window with a new 20th century view featuring many of Copenhagen's landmark towers.

As was done in 1895, a little artistic liberty was taken in placing the buildings all in one area. In the foreground can be seen the entrance to Tivoli Gardens which is 150 years old this year.

The other towers, from left to right, are Rosenborg Castle, Nicolai Church, Church of Our Lady, Copenhagen Town Hall, Marble Church, the Royal Stock Exchange, Christiansborg Castle and Our Savior Church.

The population of Copenhagen is a mere 1.8-million people spread over the entire region. But the city boasts a strong artistic heritage and a well-developed cultural infrastructure.

Copenhagen houses more than 50 museums, as many theaters, 100 music clubs and more than 200 libraries. Cultural institutions such as the National Museum of Art, Louisiana, the Royal Theater with the Royal Ballet, the New Carlsberg Glyptoteket and Tivoli are all internationally renowned.

All the above undoubtedly was taken into consideration when Copenhagen was recently named to be the 1996 Cultural Capital of Europe. Naming of such a capital started in 1985 with Athens having the first honor. Next, in order, came Florence, Amsterdam, Berlin, Paris, Glasgow, Dublin, Madrid, Antwerp, Lisbon and Luxembourg this year.

In preparation for Copenhagen's turn, several large building projects are now underway. Included are 12,000 square meters of additional space for art exhibitions at three different museums and a major extension of the Royal Library. Also underway is the interior renovation of a number of stately buildings to be used for art education and the construction of a 2000-seat concert hall at the harbor.

About The Artists

The first 100 Bing & Grøndahl Christmas plate designs are the work of only twenty-three artists, seven of them women, and most employed at one time or another by the porcelain manufactory.

Some of the artists, especially in the early days, designed only one plate; others designed varying numbers. One, the self-taught Henry Thelander, has twenty to his credit in addition to designing all of the company's Mother's Day plates beginning with the first one in 1969. Many of the artists received their early training at the Royal Academy of Fine Arts.

In the beginning the artists submitted designs in an informal competition judged by company executives. Later a theme was agreed to by the executives and they selected the artist they thought best able to carry out the motif. In modern times an artist, sometimes a free-lancer, is retained for several years.

The first three plates (1895, 1896, 1897) were the creation of Franz August Hallin (1865-1947) who received his early training as a painter in evening classes at the Royal Academy of Fine Arts. He also attended the Technical School. Employed in 1885 by Royal Copenhagen, he moved to B&G in 1895 to become chief inspector and in 1924 assistant artistic director. He retired in 1935.

Fanny Garde (1855-1928) graduated from the School of Drawing and Applied Art for Women in 1876 and taught there for the next ten years before coming to B&G, where she worked for the rest of her life. Although she designed only the 1898 plate, she created an impressive number of unique works, including suggestions for decorating dinner services, among which the Seagull is the best known. She was highly regarded by art critics of the time.

Creator of six Christmas plates between 1899 and 1915, Jens Peter Dahl-Jensen (1874-1960) began as an apprentice cabinetmaker and wood-carver before studying at the Royal Academy of Fine Arts from 1894 to 1897. He came to B&G in 1897 and worked for twenty years as a sculptor and chief modeler before being named production manager of the Norden Factory, a B&G subsidiary. In 1925 he founded his own factory for making fine porcelain.

Little is known today about five artists, each of whom apparently won single competitions for plate designs. The 1901 plate was by S. Sabra, then a "paintress" at B&G while Povl Jørgensen, a B&G painter, designed the 1908 plate.

The 1909 plate was by a Miss Aarestrup, also a painter at the company, and the following year's plate is listed as the work of a C. Ersgaard, known only as a modeler who worked under the supervision of Dahl-Jensen. Miss J. Bloch Jørgensen, another of B&G's painters, did the 1916 plate.

Margrethe Hyldahl (1881-1963) designed her first Christmas plate for B&G when she was only 22, six years before she was employed by the company in 1909. There she worked mainly on vases with landscapes and marine motifs until her death in 1963. Forty-three years were to pass after her first Christmas plate before she had a run of six straight Christmas plates, 1946 to 1951, the last one featuring the ferry *Jens Bang*.

Four other artists each are represented by just one plate. Cathinka Olsen, employed in 1896 to decorate porcelain with stylized flower motifs, had her only Christmas plate in 1904. But she found her career in 1912 when B&G began to produce art stoneware, becoming one of the leading artists in this field.

Ingeborg Plockross Irminger came to B&G right out of the Royal Academy of Fine Arts where she had studied from 1893 to 1899. Although she worked for the company for only one year her personal artistic career was thereafter intertwined with Bing & Grøndahl. Besides the 1907 plate she created more than thirty figurines and figure groups, all of which remain favorites with collectors around the world.

After retiring from the army as a Second Lieutenant in 1895, Count Harald Moltke devoted the rest of his life to art. He worked as an artist under his own signature at Royal Copenhagen during 1907-1908, then moved to B&G where he was employed until 1914. He did the 1911 plate. Fascinated by Greenland, he was a member of several expeditions to the island.

Another graduate of the Royal Academy of Fine Arts, Einar Hansen was the last of the one-plate artists. He drew portrait cartoons for Copenhagen newspapers and journals during the time he worked for B&G, 1910 to 1914. That year he went to the United States, living three years in Chicago before moving to Wheaton, Illinois. After a brief visit to Denmark in 1921, he returned to Chicago but in 1925 headed west to California where he became a teacher at the Los Angeles Art Institute and the Pasadena Art Institute.

Peter Thorvald Kristiansen Larsen, designer of the 1913 and 1914 plates, is one of four B&G artists who began art careers as house painters. While studying at the Royal Academy of Fine Arts from 1900 to 1906, he was employed by the company in 1903. Working there for many years as an artist under his own signature, he specialized in underglaze vases with landscape and marine motifs.

Johannes Achton Friis is another Royal Academy of Fine Arts graduate (1895-1899) who started out as a house painter. A very versatile artist, he is responsible for 14 Christmas plates between 1917 and 1931. He worked for B&G from 1912 to 1925. Well-known as a painter, his artistic interests included engraving, music and writing. He also participated in expeditions to Greenland.

The other two who trained initially as house painters are Hans Frithjof Immanuel Tjerne and Ove Larsen. Tjerne, who designed the 1934, 1938 and 1939 plates, also specialized in theater-painting. He worked for B&G as an underglaze painter from 1927 to 1940 then went to Nordic Films where he worked on various motion pictures.

Larsen, another Royal Academy of Fine Arts student (1908-1910) worked at B&G from 1918 to 1922 and again from 1927 until his death in 1945. His credits include nine Christmas plates: the three from 1935 to 1937 and the six from 1940 to 1945.

The 1952 and 1954 Christmas plates are the work of Børge Pramvig, an overglaze painter and supervisor of a drawing section at B&G. The 1953 plate and those from 1955 to 1962 were designed by Kjeld Bonfils, who studied architecture at the Royal Academy of Fine Arts, where he finished his career as a teacher of architecture. He was also a highly proficient jazz musician and composer of popular music.

The highly regarded Henry Thelander, designer of twenty B&G Christmas plates from 1963 to 1982, never was a B&G employee. From 1927 to 1934 he was art director at Gutenberghus, Denmark's leading advertising agency, before becoming a free-lancer. Highly regarded in advertising art circles as far away as London and Stockholm, as well as in Copenhagen, he was also a book illustrator and the creator of numerous posters.

The Christmas plates from 1983 to 1991 are the work of painter and sculptor Edvard Jensen, another of the fine art students from the Royal Academy of Fine Arts. Noted for his particular interest in Christian motifs, he has created wall paintings, ecclesiastical textiles and church silver for a number of churches in Denmark. He was also employed (1971-1977) by Royal Copenhagen.

Creator of the four most recent Christmas Plates (1992 to 1995) is Jørgen Nielsen, who has been working as a free-lancer since retiring from Royal Copenhagen in 1986. He joined RC in 1959 to train as an onglaze painter but from 1965 to 1969 he was a painter of unique underglaze vases. After time out for a two-year study tour of Japan, he returned to RC as an overglaze painter. From 1976 to 1986 Nielsen studied faience, porcelain and stoneware under noted ceramic artist Nils Thorsson. He designed the 1992 plate under the name of Jørgen Stensen but has used his own name since.

Index To Artists

1956	Kjeld Bonfils	1976	Henry Thelander
1957	Kjeld Bonfils	1977	Henry Thelander
1958	Kjeld Bonfils	1978	Henry Thelander
1959	Kjeld Bonfils	1979	Henry Thelander
1960	Kjeld Bonfils	1980	Henry Thelander
1961	Kjeld Bonfils	1981	Henry Thelander
1962	Kjeld Bonfils	1982	Henry Thelander
1963	Henry Thelander (1902-1986)	1983	Edvard Jensen (1920-)
1964	Henry Thelander	1984	Edvard Jensen
1965	Henry Thelander	1985	Edvard Jensen
1966	Henry Thelander	1986	Edvard Jensen
1967	Henry Thelander	1987	Edvard Jensen
1968	Henry Thelander	1988	Edvard Jensen
1969	Henry Thelander	1989	Edvard Jensen
1970	Henry Thelander	1990	Edvard Jensen
1971	Henry Thelander	1991	Edvard Jensen
1972	Henry Thelander	1992	Jørgen Stensen (1942-)
1973	Henry Thelander	1993	Jørgen Nielsen
1974	Henry Thelander	1994	Jørgen Nielsen
1975	Henry Thelander	1995	Jørgen Nielsen

A Brief History of Bing & Grøndahl, The National Factory of Porcelain

The Bing & Grøndahl Porcelain Factory, world-acclaimed for the quality and beauty of its products, in 1995 celebrates the centennial of the world's first commercial Christmas plate, which it originated 100 years ago. The 1895 plate, *Behind the Frozen Window*, is the first edition of what is today an important art form and popular collectors' hobby.

To begin at the beginning, Bing & Grøndahl was founded in 1853 when Copenhagen was still a small town. The factory was situated out in the country a little west of the city and, as shown on the painting on page 228, was surrounded by green fields and trees. Some of the original buildings are still in use today but the site is now completely surrounded by the city of Copenhagen.

Frederik Vilhelm Grøndahl, a young sculptor, left the employ of the Royal Copenhagen Porcelain Manufactory when that company refused to go along with his suggestion that the figurines of famed Danish sculptor Bertel Thorvaldsen be copied in "biscuit" (unglazed) porcelain. Grøndahl had been a student of Thorvaldsen.

Having considerably more ambition than money, Grøndahl took his ideas to Meyer and Jacob Bing, prosperous businessmen who owned a store which sold stationery, books and objects of art. Combining the capital and business acumen of the brothers with the artistic ideas of the young sculptor, the Bing & Grøndahl Porcelain Manufactory became a reality.

Since Denmark is practically devoid of natural resources, it was necessary from the beginning for the company to import the three main ingredients of porcelain (quartz, feldspar and kaolin) as well as coloring and firing materials.

Unfortunately, Grøndahl died about a year and half after the company was started. For several years the Bing brothers struggled to improve their products, succeeding only after skilled craftsmen were brought in from abroad. Gradually the company gained recognition in Denmark, and eventually demand for its products spread to other countries.

About 1886 Bing & Grøndahl learned the secrets of underglaze painting, then a relatively new technique of applying colors to pieces prior to firing in the kiln. Before that time the company had made many beautiful objects such as dinnerware, vases and figurines, but they had always been made in either

The original Bing & Grøndahl factory, founded in 1853 in the country outside of Copenhagen, then a small town.

"biscuit" or overglaze porcelain. In 1889 Bing & Grøndahl created quite a stir in the artistic world by showing at the Paris World Fair its new stately Heron pattern designed by Pietro Krohn. This was Europe's first complete dinnerware service in underglaze porcelain.

The company was incorporated in 1895 with the Bing family retaining the controlling interest. In the same year Harald Bing, then head of the company, conceived the idea of issuing an annual Christmas plate, using the underglaze technique. This was the first time in history that Christmas plates were produced commercially.

The first plate was placed on the market shortly before Christmas that year and bore the inscription *Jule Aften 1895* (Christmas Eve 1895). Only 400 plates were produced and sold for 50 cents each. Each year since a seven-inch blue and white plate has been made. Each new edition is eagerly anticipated by collectors in more than 70 countries.

Orders from the company's Christmas plate distributors are accepted only through October of each year. After these orders have been filled the molds are destroyed and the plates never again made, thus enhancing the value to collectors.

During the next few decades following the introduction of underglaze porcelain, the company had several great artists in its employ, including Georg Jensen, J. F. Willumsen, Effie Hegermann-Lindencrone, Fanny Garde, Hans Tegner, Kai Nielsen and Jean Rene Gauguin, son of the famous French painter Paul Gauguin. In 1888 Bing & Grøndahl received the Grand Prix of the World Exposition in Paris, thereby winning wide acclaim.

 Bing & Grøndahl exhibited stoneware for the first time in 1914. Large scale production in this field, however, has never been attempted. Instead, all efforts have been concentrated on producing a series of individual items, many of which have been acquired by museums and prominent private collectors. They started making the so-called "soft porcelain" in 1925.

The company erected a second factory in 1949 devoted exclusively to the manufacture of dinnerware. They also operated a retail outlet in the heart of Strøget, Copenhagen's world-renowned shopping district.

Bing & Grøndahl has been appointed to the royal courts of Denmark, Sweden, and Great Britain. In addition, several of the company's pieces are found in the collections of museums, including the Metropolitan Museum of Art in New York City and London's Victoria and Albert Musuem.

To commemorate the 200th anniversary of the founding of the United

The modern B&G factory, expanded many times since its humble rural beginnings, now is completely surrounded by the bustling Danish capital.

States, Bing & Grøndahl produced a Bicentennial Eagle in an edition limited to 100 pieces. Eagle No. 1 was presented to the White House in honor of the occasion.

Design and originality have remained a primary concern of the company, as evidenced by the association of artists such as Martin Hunt and the late Henning Koppel, designers of contemporary dinnerware. Bing & Grøndahl was the first manufacturer to guarantee the availability of over 20 patterns for 25 years.

From unique vases and other one-of-a-kind works of art, ranging in price up to several thousand dollars, to exquisite hand decorated dinnerware, Bing & Grøndahl has maintained the highest standards of quality and design. The same is true of their collectibles sculpted in relief and their extensive collection of porcelain figurines.

Large or small, the figurines of the more than 350-piece collection are beloved by collectors and connoisseurs of porcelain art. Created with loving care , their soft and subtle colors permanently sealed by a high gloss glaze, they capture forever children, animals and familiar situations with a charm and warmth that is a joy to behold.

Whether recreations of nature's wildlife, including birds ranging from two to 20-inches, barnyard animals, cats, dogs, polar bears, or the beautiful figurines of children captured in their many moods and poses, or the exquisite portrayal of Hans Christian Andersen, the immortal Danish storyteller, each is a work of art to be cherished.

Since the introduction of the world's first commercial Christmas plate, Bing & Grøndahl has introduced many other successful series of collectibles including Easter plaques, Mother's Day plates, Children's Day plates, Christmas in America plates and bells, Christmas tree ornaments and other items.

In 1987 Bing & Grøndahl merged with another great Danish name in porcelain, Royal Copenhagen, and today the trademark of the three towers has been reserved for collectibles. But the designs of Bing & Grøndahl continue to live -- now with the three wavy lines, the trademark of Royal Copenhagen.

A symbolic plate was produced to celebrate the historic union of Denmark's premier porcelain houses. Designed by Sven Vestergaard, the plate is 8 1/4" in diameter, and is pictured on the next page. It shows the skyline of Copenhagen which was featured on the first Bing & Grøndahl plate and the Madonna and Child from the first Royal Copenhagen plate. For the first time ever, the reverse side of this plate carried the trademarks of both houses.

The Bing & Grøndahl backstamp, depicting the three towers, is taken from the coat of arms of the city of Copenhagen and is known all over the world as the symbol of excellence. Each Bing & Grøndahl product enjoys a shared legacy of creative artistry combined with the skill of the potters craft.

The special plate symbolizing the 1987 merger shows motifs featured on the first Christmas plates produced by B&G (Copenhagen skyline) and Royal Copenhagen (Madonna and Child).

B&G Backstamps, 1853 to 1995

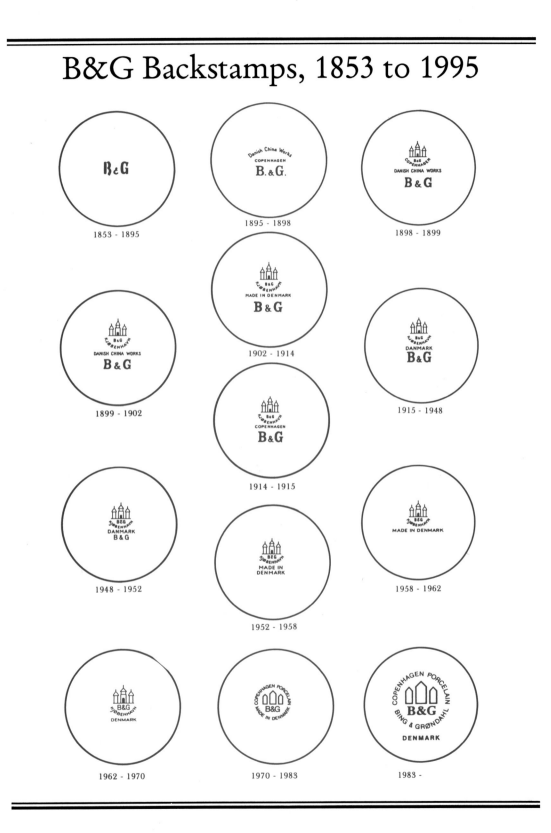

233

A Collector's Plate from Start to Finish

Few collector's plates today have the background of tradition that Bing & Grøndahl has developed over the past century.

Most of the processes involved in the creation of a Bing & Grøndahl plate require the artistry and skill of many experienced craftsmen. The first step takes place as much as two years before the plate is issued to the public.

The artist begins by drawing the image for the plate and then paints his final design. The original design is then given to a master modeler who creates the *bas relief* effect which characterizes Bing & Grøndahl Christmas plates.

Then a model of the plate design is carved and eventually cast in bronze. Working molds are made from the original. These are made of plaster of Paris and each is used for only about 20 plates before being discarded.

After an initial or bisque firing, the plate is ready for decoration. The style of decoration for which Bing & Grøndahl is most famous is the underglaze porcelain technique where the colors are applied to the bisque porcelain.

This work takes exceptional skill since the true Bing & Grøndahl blue does not really show until the final firing takes place. The decorator must learn through training and experience where to leave the color, how much to apply, where to shade and where to let the white porcelain show through.

After the decoration is applied, the plate is initialed by the artist and is ready for glazing. In this process the plate is dipped in the glaze, which after firing, produces the glaze-like surface that protects the decoration for all time. The final firing, which turns the kaolin, quartz and feldspar mixture into hard paste porcelain, takes 48 hours and subjects the plate to a temperature of 2700 degrees Fahrenheit.

The quality control inspectors then determine whether the final products match the fidelity of the original art. Any plates which fail to meet these high standards are destroyed. No "seconds" are ever offered for sale.

On each Christmas plate are the words *Jule Aften* (Christmas Eve) and the year. Each plate is pierced for hanging and is authenticated by the decorating artist's initials. The number of plates made is strictly limited and at the end of each year's production, the master model is destroyed. No more of that year's plates are ever made.

Bing & Grøndahl Christmas plates are a perfect example of handcrafted porcelain art work, truly a treasure to collect and a joy to give.

A Visit to the Studios
of the
Porcelain Plate Painters

For more than 50 women at the Bing & Grøndahl porcelain manufactory in Copenhagen, Christmas plates are more than mere tradition and taste but involve routine and rhythm as well.

To produce these highly-cherished and widely-collected plates also requires a certain talent of sensitive and nimble fingers and an unusual knowledge of how the traditional cobalt blue color behaves.

The painters sit at tables placed sideways to the factory's large windows through which the sun shines winter and summer. The workplace ambience includes a cozy mixture of green plants, personal knick-knacks and various pieces of blue painted porcelain.

On the walls, the blue collectors' plates hang in rows. On the tables and transport trolleys are Christmas plates in varying stages of production. Some are

Plate painters at work around the turn of the century.

Primitive by today's standards, the turn-of-the-century factory turned out highly acclaimed Christmas plates and other works of art. Note plate molds in the foreground.

Modern methods and modern equipment have helped make the work more pleasant while maintaining high quality standards.

still pristine white, some completely covered in blue while the motif on others is emerging in various degree.

The painters sit intent at their tasks in their protective blue smocks. The scene seems quiet and tranquil but it almost takes your breath away to look inside the "suction cabinet" where the actual work is done.

The painters work extremely fast, their hands as quick and precise as a juggler's. Spraying, brushing off, rubbing, spraying, cleaning, brushing and suddenly the dark blue surface transforms into a castle, a team of horses, children on a sled, a Christmas atmosphere.

An index finger wrapped in chamois leather carefully glides over the blue plate and the motif appears as if by magic just like the image on a photograph in

Pristine white plates are removed from molds ready for the next step in the process.

a developing tray. But it is not magic. It is a century old Danish technique enhanced by the painters' own quarter century or more of experience.

All the painters are experienced, the average length of service is 25 years. And although they work on the same Christmas plate design day-in and day-out, there is room for individuality. They plan their work day themselves so the procedure differs with each person. Everyone has their own way of decorating the plate. As each finds a special way to bring out the motif, the plates differ slightly from each other in a true measure of craftsmanship.

"It takes a few days to get familiar with a new design," explains porcelain painter Lisbeth Hansen, who recently celebrated her 27th anniversary with the company. "But I keep on until my hands get the hang of it. When it is in my bones -- in my fingertips -- I can sit and think about everything else. No, I don't

Spraying on the cobalt blue color in "suction box."

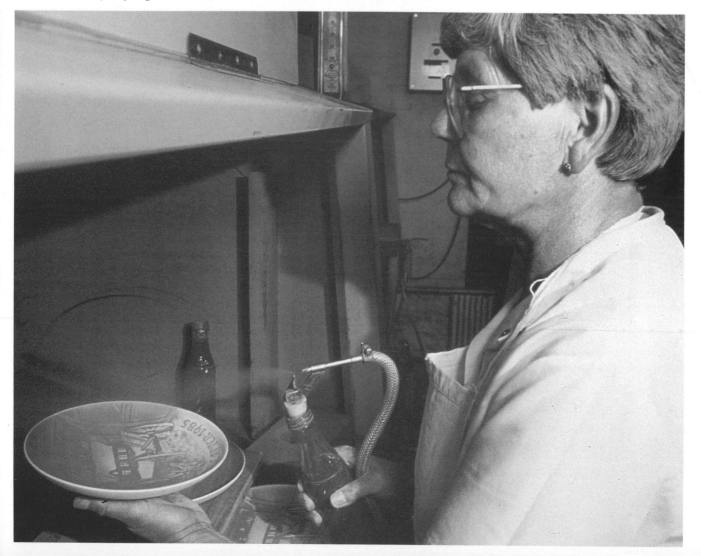

This painter is examining the color work which brings out the motif of the plate. Note the chamois leather on her thumb with which she expertly rubs the plate to bring out the color.

get tired of the work. When the cutting of a plate is good and solid it is a pleasure to decorate it."

"You need nimble fingers to bring out the many details and small surfaces," says plate painter Henny Knudsen, "The more complicated the motif, the longer it takes to make the plate." Henny has nearly 22 years of experience but still remembers how difficult it was when she first started.

A most delicate part of the operation in bringing out the blue color is in knowing how the cobalt blue will react under the heat of the kiln.

"It was so difficult that I thought I would never learn it and would be out on my ear in a fortnight. To find out how the color will lie and how to spread the color evenly was the worst. But after a while I got the hang of it," she said.

The Christmas plates are a world-famous Danish specialty. And even though the painters are proud of their work, they are also a bit surprised to learn that the Japanese are crazy about them. "But they don't even celebrate Christmas," said one. Young Italians admire the cool beauty of the plates and combine them with modern design.

Lisbeth Hansen tells about some friends who visited a home in the United States with a wall full of Christmas plates, "And on the back of one of them they found my signature!"

The blue Christmas plates are one of the results of the artistic and technical innovation in underglaze decoration by Danish porcelain manufactories in the 1880s. This underglaze *bas relief* exemplifies the play between the cutting and the color with its many blue nuances creating the motif.

The Christmas plates reflect Danish history and tradition. Christmas trees and Christmas joys with peace descending on town and country covered with white snow below a starry sky. In short: Christmas served on a plate.

A wall full of Christmas plates.

The Legend of Christmas Plates

Many, many years ago the wealthy people of Europe started a Christmas custom of giving to each of their servants a platter heaped with fruit, cookies, candies and other good things to eat.

At first the platter likely was a crude thing of wood called a trencher and very little thought was given to it. Rich and poor focused their attention on its contents hoping to bring a little cheer into the lives of the recipients by giving them especially good things to eat around the holiday season.

The servants looked forward each Christmas to receiving their gifts. Since they had few things in their homes which were not utilitarian, perhaps it was only natural that they began hanging the platters on their walls after the food was eaten. They referred to these platters as their "Christmas Plates" not to be used as ordinary trenchers, wooden plates of the time from which food was eaten.

Later the servants of one family started showing their Christmas plates to the servants of other households. When the employers realized that rivalries were developing among the servants of the various households as to who received the most attractive plates, they began giving more consideration to the platter itself.

Eventually beautiful platters were made of many materials including wood, pewter and pottery. Sometimes they were elaborately carved or painted decoratively. In fact, in an effort to outdo each other the wealthy commenced devoting more attention to the plate than to its contents. Later they began to date each platter as a record when each had been given.

Thus began the custom of making and collecting Christmas plates.

Time Line of Danish Kings and Queens

860 - 940   Gorm the Old, king over what is now Jutland, first of 53 kings and two queens to rule the 1000-year-old kingdom.

940 - 985   Harald Bluetooth, subdues all of Denmark and Norway, first to adopt Christianity; creates runic stone tribute to his parents which still exists.

985 - 1014   Sweyn Forkbeard, conquers virtually all of England and incorporates it into the Danish empire.

1014 - 1018   Harald Sweynson

1018 - 1035   Canute the Great, first Viking leader to be admitted into the "civilized fraternity of Christian kings;" extends reign over Sweden, Iceland and Greenland as well as England and Norway; empire collapses at his death at age 37.

1035 - 1042   Hardicanute, keeps a united England and Denmark until dropping dead at a wedding feast; English throne goes to Edward the Confessor.

1042 - 1047   Magnus the Good of Norway takes over Danish throne.

1047 -1076   Sweyn Estrithson, Danish son of Ulf the Jarl; fathers 19 children, the only legitimate one dies in infancy.

1076 - 1080   Harald the Hen, scornful nickname of the last ruler of the Viking Age.

1080 - 1086   Canute the Holy; Denmark's first saint, so honored after being murdered in church.

1086 - 1095   Olaf Hunger

1095 - 1103   Erik the Evergood

1103 - 1134   Niels

1134 - 1137   Erik II Emune

1137 - 1146   Erik III

1146 - 1157   Svend III is king in Zealand and Skane, Canute III is king in Jutland and Valdemar is duke in southern Jutland. After Valdemar wins the battle of Roskilde in 1157 he becomes the only king in Denmark.

1157 - 1182   Valdemar the Great; reunites the kingdom, defeats the Slavic Wend pirates with the help of his foster brother Bishop Absalon, founder of Copenhagen; establishes hereditary monarchy.

1182 - 1202	Canute IV
1202 - 1241	Valdemar II, the Victorious, conquers Pomerania, Estonia, sovereign over all Denmark, southern Sweden and entire Baltic coast; Danish flag, world's first national flag, is born in battle of Lyndanise (Lyndaniz), June 15, 1219, against Estonia; Jutland Code of 1241 grants some legal rights; civil war rages after his death.
1241 - 1250	Erik IV Ploughpenny
1250 - 1252	Abel
1252 - 1259	Christopher I
1259 - 1286	Erik V Klipping, ascends throne at age 11; enacts Denmark's Magna Carta in 1282 at Nyborg (Parliament to meet once a year, no imprisonment without trial); assassinated, Norway implicated, war begins.
1286 - 1320	Erik VI Menved, continues strife with Norway.
1320 - 1326	Christopher II, "most useless Danish monarch."
1326 - 1330	Valdemar Eriksson
1330 - 1332	Christopher II; deposed, kingdom divided.
1332 - 1340	Eight year period of strife during which there is no monarch.
1340 - 1376	Valdemar IV Atterdag (a new day), tries to restore Denmark, is defeated by Hanseatic League and Sweden and forced to flee. They approve successor.
1376 - 1387	Oluf, five-year-old son of King Haakon VI and Queen Margrethe of Norway with his mother as Regent; becomes king of Norway when his father dies in 1380; dies at age 17.
1387 - 1412	Queen Margrethe I takes power; Swedish noblemen elect her as their queen; she defeats King Albrecht of Mecklenburg who had called her "King Pantless;" in 1397 her infant nephew, Erik of Pomerania, becomes king of Denmark, Norway and Sweden but she continues to rule as Regent; Union of Kalmar in 1397 unites these three countries plus Iceland, Greenland, the Faroe Islands and part of Finland into one kingdom that lasts 126 years until Sweden and Finland secede in 1523.
1412 - 1439	Erik of Pomerania quits as unsuccessful king, becomes successful pirate.
1439 - 1448	Christopher of Bavaria, Erik's nephew, asked to suppress piracy, declines, replies "Uncle must live, too."

The Oldenburg Dynasty

1448 - 1481 Christian I

1481 - 1513 Hans, only ruler until 1972 not named Christian or Frederik.

1513 - 1523 Christian II, The Cruel, opposed by the nobility but supported by commoners, becomes hereditary King of Sweden as well; beheads 82 noblemen at coronation in "Blood Bath of Stockholm;" loses both crowns, loses battle to gain Norwegian crown and spends last 27 years imprisoned on the island of Als.

1523 - 1533 Frederik I, Duke of Holstein; revolt against Catholic Church begins.

1533 - 1559 Christian III, first Lutheran king, beats off attempt to restore Christian II; presides over Reformation in Denmark and Norway; ends civil strife.

1559 - 1588 Frederik II, fails in bloody battle to take over Sweden.

1588 - 1648 Christian IV, the Builder King; establishes trading companies; equips army and navy; encourages art; lays out new cities in Denmark and Norway; builds country's finest palaces, churches; also called The Sailor King for his interest in things nautical; popular hero then and now; suffers crushing defeat by Germany and Sweden in 30 Years' War.

249

1648 - 1670 Frederik III, secret constitution returns power to the monarchy.

1670 - 1699 Christian V, plans many castles, builds only a few, regarded as "shallow, weak and vain."

1699 - 1730 Frederik IV, elopes with 19-year-old Anna Sophie Reventlow in 1712 while still married to Queen Louise, but marries her legally when Louise dies in 1721; abolishes serfdom; founds 240 elementary schools in Denmark; builds the lovely Fredensborg Palace.

1730 - 1746 Christian VI, last of the "Builder Kings;" makes church attendance compulsory; bans theater, dancing and celebrations.

1746 - 1766 Frederik V, one of most popular Danish kings; ends Puritanism at court; builds Amalienborg Castle and Square; builds Frederik's Hospital; establishes academies for artists, sculptors, painters and architects.

1766 - 1808 Christian VII, makes Amalienborg Palace the official royal residence after fire in 1794 destroyed Christiansborg Castle.

1808 - 1839	Frederik VI, regent for 20 years before ascending throne; dragged into Napoleonic conflicts; English bombard Copenhagen in 1808; Norway ceded to Sweden in Treaty of Kiel reducing Denmark to about present size; abolishes Stavsbaand law which had tied peasants to landed estates.
1839 - 1848	Christian VIII, gives permission to establish Tivoli Park.
1848 - 1863	Frederik VII, renounces absolute monarchy, signs new constitution June 5, 1849 establishing two-house parliament and granting freedom of speech, religion, personal liberty.
1863 - 1906	Christian IX, with 10 children becomes Europe's father-in-law.
1906 - 1912	Frederik VIII
1912 - 1947	Christian X, reign spans World Wars I and II; suffrage for women in 1915; Iceland becomes independent in 1944; voting age lowered from 35 to 25; social reforms begin; very popular monarch.
1947 - 1972	Frederik IX, also popular, continues reforms; signs new constitution on June 5, 1953 creating single chamber parliament and making it possible for a woman to succeed to the throne.
1972 -	Queen Margrethe II, well-known painter, illustrator of several books, and designer of figurines; Denmark joins the European Common Market.

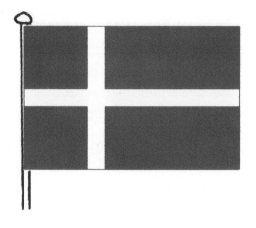

The Story of the Danish Flag

The flag of Denmark, dating back to June 15, 1219, is the oldest national flag in the world and the story of its origin is most unusual.

Valdemar the Victorious, king of Denmark from 1202 to 1241, extended Denmark's domain by conquest of the Baltic coast. During the battle of Lyndanise, one of the major battles in a war with Estonia, the Danes found themselves greatly outnumbered and almost completely surrounded.

As they retreated many of the soldiers and the clergy among them knelt to pray. The legend has it that as they prayed to God for guidance, a red banner emblazoned with a white cross came floating gently down through the clouds. A heavenly voice was heard to tell the Danes to take up this banner and return to the battle.

This they did, and the Estonians were quickly conquered.

This miraculous banner was named the *Dannebrog* (Dane's Cloth) and for the next 300 years this original banner was carried in all their many wars. It eventually disappeared during a battle against Germany, but replicas of the original are still used as the Danish national flag.

The Danish people are proud of their flag and fly it often. They display it on holidays and on birthdays: the king's, their own, their children's, their grandchildren's, their grandparents' and on silver wedding anniversaries as well. They also use small flags as decorations on their Christmas trees.

Price Guide to Bing & Grøndahl Christmas Plates

The prices listed are a reflection of transactions reported by a number of retailers and mail-order houses dealing in these collectibles. The survey was taken in mid-November, 1994 and reflects asking prices as well as actual transactions to that date. Prices given varied greatly and collectors are cautioned that a check of the marketplace will reveal prices both lower and higher than those listed here. It is safe to assume, however, based on the historical record, that prices will be higher with each passing year.

Date	Title	Artist	Issue Price	Current Value
1895	Behind the Frozen Window	Hallin	0.50	$7,500.00
1896	New Moon Over Snow-Covered Trees	Hallin	0.50	3,186.00
1897	Christmas Meal of the Sparrows	Hallin	0.75	2,000.00
1898	Christmas Roses and Christmas Star	Garde	0.75	978.00
1899	The Crows Enjoying Christmas	Dahl-Jensen	0.75	2,500.00
1900	Church Bells Chiming in Christmas	Dahl-Jensen	0.75	1,600.00
1901	Three Wise Men from the East	Sabra	1.00	510.00
1902	Interior of a Gothic Church	Dahl-Jensen	1.00	480.00
1903	Happy Expectation of the Children	Hyldahl	1.00	429.00
1904	Copenhagen from Frederiksberg Hill	Olsen	1.00	179.00
1905	Anxiety of the Coming Christmas Night	Dahl-Jensen	1.00	179.00
1906	Sleighing to Church on Christmas Eve	Dahl-Jensen	1.00	144.00
1907	The Little Match Girl	Irminger	1.00	150.00
1908	St. Petri Church of Copenhagen	P. Jørgensen	1.00	108.00
1909	Happiness Over the Yule Tree	Aarestrup	1.50	145.00
1910	The Old Organist	Ersgaard	1.50	134.00
1911	First Sung by Angels to Shepherds	Moltke	1.50	132.00
1912	Going to Church on Christmas Eve	Hansen	1.50	110.00
1913	Bringing Home the Yule Tree	T. Larsen	1.50	132.00
1914	Amalienborg Castle, Copenhagen	T. Larsen	1.50	105.00
1915	Dog's Double Meal on Christmas Eve	Dahl-Jensen	1.50	156.00
1916	Christmas Prayer of the Sparrows	J. Jørgensen	1.50	90.00
1917	Arrival of the Christmas Boat	Friis	1.50	90.00
1918	Fishing Boat Home for Christmas	Friis	1.50	90.00
1919	Outside the Lighted Window	Friis	2.00	90.00
1920	Hare in the Snow	Friis	2.00	90.00
1921	Pigeons in the Castle Court	Friis	2.00	89.00
1922	Star of Bethlehem	Friis	2.00	95.00
1923	Royal Hunting Castle, the *Eremitage*	Friis	2.00	116.00

Date	Title	Artist	Issue Price	Current Value
1924	Lighthouse in Danish Waters	Friis	2.50	$84.00
1925	The Child's Christmas	Friis	2.50	96.00
1926	Churchgoers on Christmas Day	Friis	2.50	93.00
1927	Skating Couple	Friis	2.50	117.00
1928	Eskimos and their Church in Greenland	Friis	2.50	75.00
1929	Fox Outside Farm on Christmas Eve	Friis	2.50	105.00
1930	Yule Tree, Town Hall Sq., Copenhagen	Flügenring	2.50	141.00
1931	Arrival of the Christmas Train	Friis	2.50	96.00
1932	Lifeboat at Work	Flügenring	2.50	99.00
1933	The Korsør-Nyborg Ferry	Flügenring	3.00	81.00
1934	Church Bell in Tower	Tjerne	3.00	112.00
1935	The Lillebelt Bridge	O. Larsen	3.00	120.00
1936	Royal Guard, Amalienborg Castle	O. Larsen	3.00	81.00
1937	Arrival of Christmas Guests	O. Larsen	3.00	108.00
1938	Lighting the Candles	Tjerne	3.00	206.00
1939	Ole Lock-Eye, the Sandman	Tjerne	3.00	195.00
1940	Delivering Christmas Letters	O. Larsen	4.00	272.00
1941	Horses Enjoying Christmas Meal	O. Larsen	4.00	364.00
1942	Danish Farm on Christmas Night	O. Larsen	4.00	231.00
1943	The Ribe Cathedral	O. Larsen	5.00	316.00
1944	The Sorgenfri Castle	O. Larsen	5.00	177.00
1945	The Old Water Mill	O. Larsen	5.00	196.00
1946	Memorial to Danish WWII Sailors	Hyldahl	5.00	136.00
1947	The Dybbøl Mill	Hyldahl	5.00	192.00
1948	Watchman, Copenhagen Town Hall	Hyldahl	5.50	116.00
1949	19th Century Danish Soldier	Hyldahl	5.50	124.00
1950	Kronborg Castle at Elsinore	Hyldahl	5.50	195.00
1951	Jens Bang Passenger Boat	Hyldahl	6.00	164.00
1952	Old Copenhagen Canals	Pramvig	6.00	155.00
1953	King's Boat in Greenland Waters	Bonfils	7.00	140.00
1954	Hans Christian Andersen Birthplace	Pramvig	7.50	172.00
1955	The Kalundborg Church	Bonfils	8.00	188.00
1956	Christmas in Copenhagen	Bonfils	8.50	153.00
1957	Christmas Candles	Bonfils	9.00	204.00
1958	Santa Claus	Bonfils	9.50	204.00
1959	Christmas Eve	Bonfils	10.00	196.00
1960	Danish Christmas Church	Bonfils	10.00	204.00
1961	Winter Harmony	Bonfils	10.50	141.00
1962	Winter Night	Bonfils	11.00	112.00
1963	The Christmas Elf	Thelander	11.00	208.00
1964	Fir Tree and the Hare	Thelander	11.50	78.00
1965	Bringing Home the Christmas Tree	Thelander	12.00	88.00
1966	Home for Christmas	Thelander	12.00	69.00
1967	Sharing the Joy of Christmas	Thelander	13.00	60.00

Date	Title	Artist	Issue Price	Current Value
1968	Christmas in Church	Thelander	14.00	$56.00
1969	Arrival of Christmas Guests	Thelander	14.00	56.00
1970	Pheasants in the Snow at Christmas	Thelander	14.50	54.00
1971	Christmas at Home	Thelander	15.00	25.00
1972	Christmas in Greenland	Thelander	16.50	32.00
1973	Country Christmas	Thelander	19.50	45.00
1974	Christmas in the Village	Thelander	22.00	45.00
1975	Christmas at the Old Water Mill	Thelander	27.50	40.00
1976	Christmas Welcome	Thelander	27.50	42.00
1977	Copenhagen Christmas	Thelander	29.50	33.00
1978	A Christmas Tale	Thelander	32.00	49.00
1979	White Christmas	Thelander	36.50	49.00
1980	Christmas in the Woods	Thelander	42.50	50.00
1981	Christmas Peace	Thelander	49.50	60.00
1982	The Christmas Tree	Thelander	54.50	72.00
1983	Christmas in the Old Town	Jensen	54.50	86.00
1984	The Christmas Letter	Jensen	54.50	79.00
1985	Christmas Eve at the Farmhouse	Jensen	54.50	72.00
1986	Silent Night, Holy Night	Jensen	54.50	100.00
1987	The Snowman's Christmas Eve	Jensen	59.50	78.00
1988	H. C. Andersen, King's Garden	Jensen	59.50	81.00
1989	Christmas Anchorage	Jensen	59.50	100.00
1990	Changing the Guard, Fredensborg	Jensen	64.50	90.00
1991	Copenhagen Stock Exchange	Jensen	69.50	100.00
1992	The Pastor's Christmas	Stensen	69.50	85.00
1993	Father Christmas in Copenhagen	Nielsen	72.50	75.00
1994	A Day at the Deer Park	Nielsen	72.50	72.50
1995	Copenhagen, City of Towers	Nielsen	74.50	

Plate Purchase Record

Date	Item	Vendor	Price